I0814224

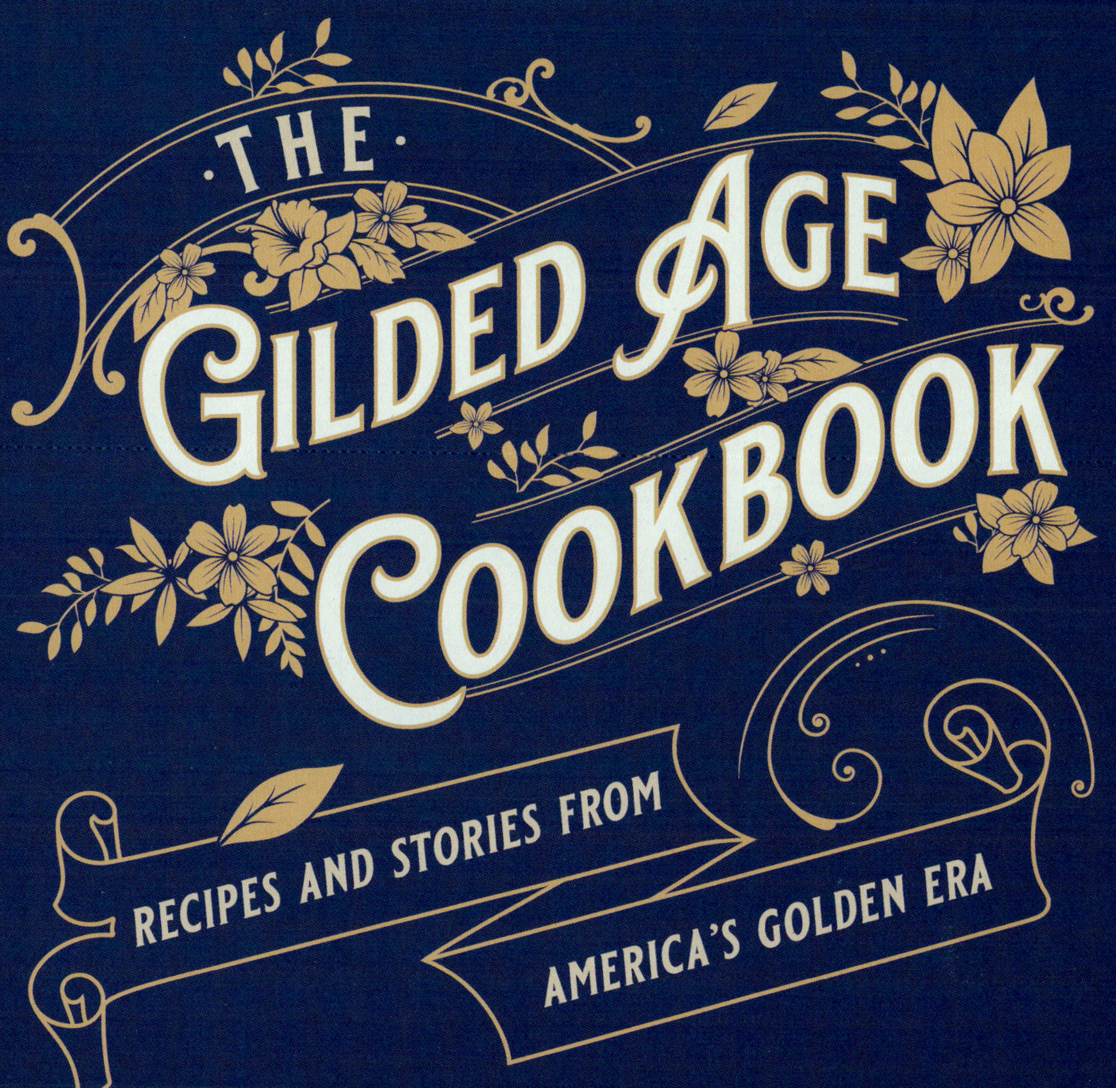

BECKY LIBOUREL DIAMOND

with

Photography by **HEATHER RAUB** of FrontRoom Images

Food styling by **DAN MACEY** of dantasticfood

Foreword by **CHEF WALTER STAIB**,
host/executive producer of *A Taste of History*

Globe
Pequot

Essex, Connecticut

Globe
Pequot

An imprint of The Globe Pequot Publishing Group, Inc.
64 South Main Street
Essex, CT 06426
www.globepequot.com

Distributed by NATIONAL BOOK NETWORK

British Library Cataloguing in Publication Information available

Library of Congress Cataloging-in-Publication Data
Names: Diamond, Becky Libourel, author.
Title: The Gilded Age cookbook : recipes and stories from America's golden era / Becky Libourel Diamond with photography by Heather Raub of FrontRoom Images ; food styling by Dan Macey of Dantasticfood ; foreword by Chef Walter Staib, host/executive producer of A Taste of History.
Description: Essex, Connecticut : Globe Pequot, [2023] | Includes bibliographical references and index. | Summary: "A cookbook featuring rich soups, juicy roasts, and luscious desserts come to life through historic images and artistic photography. Gilded Age details and entertaining stories of celebrities from the era—the Vanderbilts, Astors, Carnegies, and Rockefellers—are melded with historic menus and recipes updated for modern kitchens"— Provided by publisher.
Identifiers: LCCN 2022058831 (print) | LCCN 2022058832 (ebook) | ISBN 9781493069453 (cloth) | ISBN 9781493069460 (epub)
Subjects: LCSH: Cooking, American. | Desserts. | Dinners and dining—United States—19th century—History. | LCGFT: Cookbooks.
Classification: LCC TX715 .D54 2023 (print) | LCC TX715 (ebook) | DDC 641.5973—dc23/eng/20221214
LC record available at https://lccn.loc.gov/2022058831
LC ebook record available at https://lccn.loc.gov/2022058832

Printed in India

CONTENTS

FOREWORD

I began my career in the Black Forest at the age of four, peeling garlic in my uncle's restaurant, Gasthaus Zum Buckenberg. There was never any doubt in my mind as to what my future profession and lifelong passion would be.

This entrepreneurial spirit led to the creation of Concepts By Staib, Ltd., a global restaurant management and hospitality consulting firm, which has successfully conceptualized and implemented more than 650 restaurants worldwide.

After several successful years on my own, I went looking for a property to expand the consulting business. In 1992, I learned that Philadelphia's City Tavern, a reincarnation of the fabled colonial-era restaurant in Philadelphia, had closed and was looking for a new proprietor.

First built in 1773, City Tavern served as the unofficial White House when Philadelphia was the capital of the United States. My fascination for American history was born here and led to my desire to rehabilitate this treasure of our nation's founders.

It became my passion to authentically reintroduce the culinary prowess present in eighteenth-century American cuisine but somehow lost in subsequent years. A vision emerged that guests could enjoy a "taste" of the past and share the atmosphere of gentility and food cheer that our nation's founders appreciated.

A common misconception is that the American cuisine of previous centuries was dull, flavorless, and limited. That assumption couldn't be further from the truth, especially in the city of Philadelphia. In the eighteenth century, it was the largest city in the New World, the second-largest city in the British Empire, and home to open-air markets that offered an endless bounty of the area.

Not surprisingly, minimalist cuisine was not the fashion in such an atmosphere. Dinner at City Tavern or any of the fine homes of Philadelphia, such as Strawberry Mansion, the Hill-Physick House, Bishop White's House, or the Harriton Estate, could include twenty or more different dishes.

For the "common citizen" in the colonies, the abundance of meals was less extravagant, but as John Adams reported to his wife, Abigail, even "plain Quakers" served ducks, hams, chicken, and beef at a single sitting. In Europe, only royalty could hunt, but in America, that opportunity was available to anyone. The abundance of seafood and game was part of William Penn's original appeal to Quakers in leaving England to make the dangerous journey to the New World. Food, in general, became a part of the new American colonists' identity and culture.

This concept of eighteenth-century gourmet cuisine inspired me to pen the *City Tavern Cookbook*, which chronicles the historical and cultural influences that produced such inspired culinary performances.

I continued to evolve this devotion into *A Taste of History*, a TV cooking series on PBS and Amazon Prime that explores America's culinary beginnings from the Birthplace of American Cuisine. The viewer steps back in time and gets to know the founders of our country through the food they ate and the recipes they prepared.

I see this same adoration and dedication to historic cuisine in my good friend Becky Libourel Diamond, a brilliant scholar of eighteenth- and nineteenth-century American recipes. I'm privileged to pass the torch to her as she takes you on a journey of America's Gilded Age, a time of great affluence when American business took off on a grand scale and life was accelerating at a rapid pace of luxurious modernization. Innovations changed how people lived, traveled the world, and gained access to previously unheard-of appliances, utensils, and ingredients. This book tells the stories of the most important events and people of the "Golden Era" of American history through food, constructing an array of dazzling menus that reflect its savory history.

There is no more delectable way to learn or return to the Gilded Age than through the delicious dishes in *The Gilded Age Cookbook.* Transport back in time to lavish banquet tables set with snowy white linen tablecloths, delicate china, and sparkling crystal glasses, and revel in this step-by-step guide to enjoying such singular delights right in your very own home.

Chef Walter Staib

Host/Executive Producer, *A Taste of History*

President, Concepts by Staib, Ltd.

Former Proprietor, City Tavern Restaurant

TIPS ON INGREDIENTS AND TECHNIQUES

Several recipes in this cookbook call for mayonnaise. Feel free to try the homemade recipe featured in the Waldorf Salad (chapter 3, page 113), or use your favorite jarred variety.

Several recipes call for ground nutmeg. If you can, purchase a jar of whole nutmegs and grate them with a fine grater yourself as you need them. It is much fresher tasting!

Rosewater and orange flower water (sometimes called orange blossom water) can be found online or in specialty markets like Whole Foods and sometimes the international section of supermarkets. I usually use Al Wadi brand (Cortas and Sadaf are other brands).

WHIPPING EGG WHITES

Room-temperature eggs will whip easier, so for best results separate eggs when they are cold and then let them come to room temperature, about 30 minutes. Always use a clean mixing bowl made from glass, stainless steel, or copper (not plastic). When whipping egg whites with an electric mixer, start on a low speed and then increase speed when they start to look foamy. The length of time depends on the stage you need for the recipe as well as other factors including the age of the eggs and the temperature and humidity of your kitchen. Use this sight guide to help:

- **FOAMY/FLUFFY** The egg whites will look foamy with small bubbles. At this point, some recipes call for cream of tartar or another acidic ingredient to help boost volume.

- **SOFT PEAKS** The egg whites hold their shape and droop over to the side when the beater is lifted up. If making a meringue or another sweet recipe, this is the stage to add the sugar.
- **FIRM PEAKS** The egg whites will keep their shape when the beater is lifted up.
- **STIFF PEAKS** The tips of the egg whites will look smooth and glossy and stand straight up both on the beater(s) and on the surface.

MAKING WHIPPED CREAM

A chilled bowl and beater(s) will whip cream quicker and more efficiently, so when making whipped cream, it's best to put the mixing bowl and beater(s) in the freezer for at least 15 minutes.

RE-CREATING RECIPES

All the recipes have been re-created to reflect modern ingredients.

HOSTING YOUR OWN GILDED AGE–THEMED MEAL

Don't worry if you don't have access to authentic Gilded Age dishes, glassware, and serving pieces. Mix and match family heirlooms and vintage items from yard sales, thrift stores, etc., or simply use whatever you have and make it your own!

INTRODUCTION

There are few more ancient institutions than the dinner table, or any which has so suddenly become picturesque and luxurious beyond the fashion of the immediate past.

—"A MODERN DINNER TABLE," *HARPER'S BAZAAR*, 1883

The 1870s ushered in the era of the Gilded Age, a time frame in America's history that glittered with magnificent wealth on the surface, but bubbled underneath with corruption and social issues. A satirical phrase conceived by writer Mark Twain in his novel by the same name, the Gilded Age painted a picture of what was happening in the United States during the last few decades of the nineteenth century. Much of the period's extreme prosperity was a direct result of post–Civil War industrial innovations and booming enterprises, which fueled the greed of captains of industry who benefited from the technological progress. And while the rich got richer, countless others worked long hours doing manual labor to help propel these advances forward, often living in squalid, overcrowded tenements.

The excessive opulence and novel inventions spawned new opportunities, particularly for cooking-related endeavors. Culinary roles for women and minorities became more significant during this time, and revolutionary technologies such as kitchen appliances and canned goods were game changers. An ever-expanding network of trains and fast steamships increased the availability of foods such as beef, fish, eggs, fruits, and vegetables, and the introduction of the groundbreaking Pullman Dining Car allowed people to dine in grandeur while traveling by rail.

Philanthropy among the rich helped fund cooking classes for both affluent ladies and working women. The success of these cooking schools paved the way for a variety of cooking instruction models, including the home economics movement and culinary training as a viable career path. Cooking became a form of entertainment, with culinary experts presenting cooking techniques in front of packed audiences decades before cooking shows became a television staple.

The restaurant and hotel industries also profited greatly during the Gilded Age, experiencing explosive growth in order to keep up with the steady stream of people flowing into large cities such as New York. These included stylish and sophisticated establishments such as Delmonico's that catered to the wealthy, as well as basic eateries for the growing middle class. Men congregated at exclusive eating clubs, where they could meet, share information, and socialize while enjoying a good meal, a concept borrowed from London's famed "gentlemen's clubs."

Ladies busied themselves by calling on each other and hosting ladies' luncheons and afternoon tea parties as a way to exchange civilities, gain support for charitable causes, showcase the latest fashions and trends, and meet social obligations. In the evenings, elaborate multi-course dinner parties were common.

As more families began to move farther away from the hustle, bustle, and uncleanliness of city business districts, the time for the dinner meal was pushed back to early evening when the man of the house returned from work and could participate in the socializing. Lavish banquet dinners and debutante balls hosted by high society magnates such as Ward McAllister, Caroline Astor, and Mamie Fish flourished during the Gilded Age as a way to flaunt wealth and define who was "in." Luxurious wedding breakfasts were catered affairs that frequently featured two different menus—one for the wedding party and one for the guests.

In the warmer months, social activities moved outside, with picnics, ice cream socials, strawberry fetes and festivals, and beach excursions serving as popular themes. Many of the Gilded Age über-rich moved their summer entertaining to Newport, Rhode Island, hosting exclusive golf and tennis luncheons, balls,

Supper tables with buffet, Mrs. Beeton's Book of Household Management, *1907.* WIKIMEDIA COMMONS

and dinner parties. Saratoga Springs, New York, and beach resorts such as Long Branch and Cape May, New Jersey, were also trendy seasonal locales. All of these spots would have been a refreshing relief from the stifling heat and humidity of cities like New York and Philadelphia.

The holiday season was another reason for celebratory gatherings, with both Thanksgiving and Christmas typically the most carefully planned meals of the year for many families. Meals featured elaborate multi-course menus ranging from oysters on the half shell and turkey with all the trimmings to sugar plums and plum pudding. Festivities extended into New Year's Day and Twelfth Night (January 6), a time for parties, games, and feasting on rich Twelfth Night Cake.

All of these factors helped define the Gilded Age and its significance to America's culinary history. Massive urban growth occurred not only in New York, but also in Philadelphia and Chicago, as well as cities out West such as Denver and San Francisco. The railroad helped connect these growing cities and boost industry, leading to a surging upper and middle class. This included a small but vital African-American elite who socialized in similar ways as white

Dinner party table, Mrs. Beeton's Book of Household Management, *1907. WIKIMEDIA COMMONS*

society. The upshot was that more and more people had the wherewithal to live in comfort and style. The unique types of food they sought reflected the era's marked changes in dining habits as they navigated a complex and changing world. The style and excessiveness of this period continue to be a source of wonder and fascination for us today.

The Gilded Age Cookbook reconstructs this era of lavish banquet tables set with snowy white linen tablecloths, delicate china, and sparkling crystal glasses. Gilded Age details are melded with historic menus and recipes updated for contemporary kitchens, allowing modern cooks to duplicate meals and gatherings from the past while celebrating today. Enjoy traveling back in time to the Gilded Age!

Mark Twain's Homesick Food

Mark Twain, the writer who coined the phrase "The Gilded Age," in his 1873 book by the same name, was also someone who enjoyed food. After returning from a trip touring Europe for a year in 1878 and complaining about the hotel meals he encountered there, Twain compiled a "bill of fare" of American foods for which he was homesick. He advised other American travelers to copy his list "and carry it along" on their own journey to remember what awaited them when they return home.

The list is a nice snapshot of what was popular food at the time and available on menus all across the country. It's interesting to note that Twain yearns for very specific foods from precise locations—a likely reflection of local specialties and what was considered American regional delicacies. And like today, he complains of not being able to get ice water in Europe similar to what he was accustomed to in America.

HERE IS HIS LIST AS HE WROTE IT:

Radishes. Baked apples with cream.

Fried oysters; stewed oysters. Frogs.

American coffee, with real cream.

American butter.

Fried chicken, Southern style.

Porter-house steak.

Saratoga potatoes.

Broiled chicken, American style.

Hot biscuits, Southern style.

Hot wheat-bread, Southern style.

Hot buckwheat cakes.

American toast. Clear Maple syrup.

Virginia bacon, broiled.

Blue points, on the half shell.

Cherry-stone clams.

San Francisco mussels, steamed.

Oyster soup. Clam soup.

Philadelphia Terapin soup.

Oysters roasted in shell—
Northern style.

Soft shell crabs. Connecticut shad.

Baltimore perch.

Brook trout, from Sierra Nevadas.

Lake trout, from Tahoe.

Sheep-head and croakers, from New Orleans.

Black bass from Mississippi.

American roast beef.

Roast turkey, Thanksgiving style.

Cranberry sauce. Celery.

Roast wild turkey. Woodcock.

Canvas-back-duck, from Baltimore.

Prairie hens, from Illinois.

Missouri partridges, broiled.

Possum. Coon.

Boston bacon and beans.

Bacon and greens, Southern style.

Hominy. Broiled onions. Turnips.

Pumpkin. Squash. Asparagus.

Butter beans. Sweet potatoes.

Lettuce. Succotash. String beans.

Mashed potatoes. Catsup.

Broiled potatoes, in their skins.

New potatoes, minus the skins.

Early rose potatoes, roasted in the ashes, Southern style, served hot.

Sliced tomatoes, with sugar and vinegar.

Stewed tomatoes.

Green corn, cut from the ear, and served with butter and pepper.

Hot corn-pone, with chitlings, Southern style.

Hot hoe-cake, Southern style.

Hot egg bread, Southern style.

Buttermilk. Iced sweet milk.

Apple dumplings, with real cream.

Apple pie. Apple fritters.

Apple puffs, Southern style.

Peach cobbler, Southern style.

Peach pie. American mince pie.

Pumpkin pie. Squash pie.

All sorts of American pastry.

Fresh American fruit of all sorts, including strawberries which are not to be doled out as if they were jewelry, but in a more liberal way.

Ice-water—not prepared in the ineffectual goblet, but in a sincere and capable refrigerator.

Contributed by food historian and culinary stylist Dan Macey

Chapter One

Culinary Innovations

THE RAILROADS AND DINING

Boston Brown Bread

Potage Purée

Spinach à la Crème

Broiled Steak

Blueberry Cake

COOKING SCHOOLS / FOOD DEMOS

Roast Chicken, au Jus

Simply Scallops

Crispy Potatoes à la Parisienne

Cream Puffs

KITCHEN INNOVATIONS

Chocolate Macaroons

Dolly Varden Cake

Lemon Meringue Pie

Aunt Lizzie's Pineapple Pie

The culinary science is a progressive one . . . many important discoveries are made every day, and new processes devised that add a new spice to life's enjoyments.

—MRS. GRACE TOWNSEND, *DINING ROOM AND KITCHEN*, 1902

THE GILDED AGE was a time of prosperous industrial and technological growth. An ever-expanding network of trains and fast steamships increased the availability of many foods, including beef, fish, eggs, fruits, and vegetables. The railroad was particularly significant for its role in making millionaire industry tycoons, in addition to allowing the transport of goods and upscale travel and dining opportunities. Cooking schools started to become more practical and inclusive, and innovative gadgets and ingredients such as the rotary eggbeater and baking powder made the cook's job easier. This chapter highlights the inventions that significantly impacted America's gastronomic journey by freeing up time in the kitchen and introducing new food types and techniques.

THE RAILROADS AND DINING

Many of the glittering Gilded Age mansions of New York and Newport were built by the railroads. Fortunes were made by the industry titans who created and controlled the American railway system, leading to the excessive lifestyle so prominent during the era. People and goods could travel greater distances in much less time. Perishable foods such as meats, dairy products, and fresh produce became much more popular and accessible following the introduction of refrigerated railcars in 1871, upping the fine-dining game for the wealthy and introducing a wider range of food options to the growing middle class.

GILDED AGE RAILROAD TYCOONS

Following the Civil War, America underwent a railroad boom, as the race to lay down track to shuttle people and goods around the country heated up. Railroad tycoons saw this investment opportunity and relentlessly expanded rail and other transportation systems, often building new railways right next to established ones. Some bought up lines, inflated the stock, and then sold it at a profit. These men are well known to the Gilded Age roster, with names such as James Hill, Jay and George Gould, Cornelius and William Vanderbilt, Edward Harriman, Henry Villard, August Belmont, Robert Goelet, and Collis P. Huntington. These railroad robber barons built much of the US rail network, but unfortunately their ruthless race to accumulate wealth included the exploitation of workers, shady deals, and general disregard of standard business rules and laws. Eventually their greed for profits led to railroad regulation.

A man by the name of George Pullman revolutionized rail travel in 1868 when he debuted the dining car. Pullman had already introduced a drastically improved version of the sleeping car in 1865 and an innovative hotel car in 1867, but it was undoubtedly the dining car that changed the game for rail travel. Appropriately named the *Delmonico*, it featured an extensive menu of fine-dining options served on elegant china, crystal, and silver; a luxurious setting; and impeccable service. The wine list was extensive, with more than

When traveling from Chicago to Omaha en route to California in 1872, travel guide writer Charles Nordoff said he expected to find the dining car "greasy, a little untidy, and with a smell of the kitchen. . . . But in fact it was neat, as nicely fitted, as trim and cleanly, as though Delmonico had furnished it; and though the kitchen may be in the forward end of the car, so perfect is the ventilation that there is not even the faintest odor of cooking."

—*HARPERS NEW MONTHLY MAGAZINE*, 1872

fifty wines, as well as brandy, port, and Madeira. The *Delmonico* had everything that could be expected at an expensive restaurant.

It required a great deal of ingenuity to pull off such a feat. The compact kitchen (just eight by eight feet) contained a water tank, sink, range, tables, and a pantry for storage. Meats, fruits, vegetables, and other fresh foods were stored in a large icebox underneath. In early versions of the Pullman Dining Car, the kitchen was situated in the center, with dining areas on either side. Pullman designed it this way at first to try to make the cooking smells less obtrusive and the dining

Pullman Dining Car "Continental."

DINNER.

EN ROUTE, SEPTEMBER 15, 1888.

Consomme, a la Royale — Brunoise
Baked Bluefish, a l'Anglaise
Parisienne Potatoes

Boiled Capon, with Mocaroni

Roast Beef — English Rib Ends of Beef with Browned Potatoes
Roast Spring Lamb, Mint Sauce
Young Turkey, with Dressing

Fricandeau of Veal, a la Macedoine
Saute of Chicken Giblets, aux Champignons
Apple Fritters, au Glase

Lobster Salad — Lettuce Salad

Spanish Olives — Raw Tomatoes
Chow Chow — Pickled Onions — Girkins

Boiled Potatoes — New Potatoes in Cream — Mashed Potatoes
Lima Beans — Summer Squash
Green Corn

Cottage Pudding, Wine Sauce — Green Apple Pie

Fruit — Watermelon
Ice Cream — Assorted Cake — Preserved Fruit
Marmalade — Raisins
English, Graham and Oatmeal Wafers

Roquefort and Edam Cheese — Bent's Crackers
Cafe Noir

MEALS, ONE DOLLAR.

Table Water from the Silurian Springs, Waukesha

Dinner Menu, New York & Chicago Limited Pullman Dining Car, 1888. NEW YORK PUBLIC LIBRARY

Efficiency on the Pullman Car

The "Pullman loaf" was a straight-edged style of bread served on Pullman Dining Cars. It was made in a rectangular pan with a sliding lid that kept the bread in shape as it baked and produced a delicately textured bread with very little crust. Based on the French *pain de mie*, a white bread often used to make sandwiches, canapés, and croutons, the symmetrical shape was easier to store in the minimal kitchen space available.

areas more accessible from other cars, although in later versions the kitchen was moved to one end.

Each dining area could seat a total of forty-eight people divided among six tables for four. Upon entering this luxurious car, diners were greeted with gleaming silver-trimmed mahogany woodwork and silver candle sconces. Tapestry blinds covered the windows for privacy and light filtering. Large chandeliers hung from the ceiling, flanked by colorful stained glass panels. Plush carpeting and velvet chairs completed the experience of dining in comfort and style.

One European rail traveler who marveled at the innovative Pullman dining car wrote in 1879: "The waiter spreads your table with a neat linen cloth, and touching a spring, opens the mirror between windows at your side, disclosing to view the silver service belonging to each quartette of diners. Then a savory steak of beef or antelope, mountain trout or broiled chicken are placed before you smoking hot. Wine, tea, coffee or fresh milk are at your command."

—C. DEAN, *THE WORLD'S FAIR CITY AND HER ENTERPRISING SONS*

The dining car served breakfast, lunch, and dinner, and all meals had extensive, plentiful choices. Breakfast, which was 75 cents in 1882, featured eight types of bread (including four kinds of toast—dry, dipped, cream, and buttered), broiled meats such as mutton chops and sirloin steak, game, oysters, fried meats, eggs, relishes, fruits, and vegetables. Dinner typically ranged from 75 cents to $1 and included up to eighty dishes, with items such as oysters, soup, baked fish, game pie, shrimp salad, and in-season vegetables, as well as desserts ranging from blanc mange, apple pie, assorted cake, and ice cream to fruit and cheese.

Maintaining such a high level of service came at an extreme cost. Dining cars were not only expensive to build, but also needed a large staff and pricey equipment. Pullman hired recently freed enslaved housemen as dining car employees for their expertise and

Chicago, Burlington and Quincy Railroad dining car, 1880.

© GETTY IMAGES

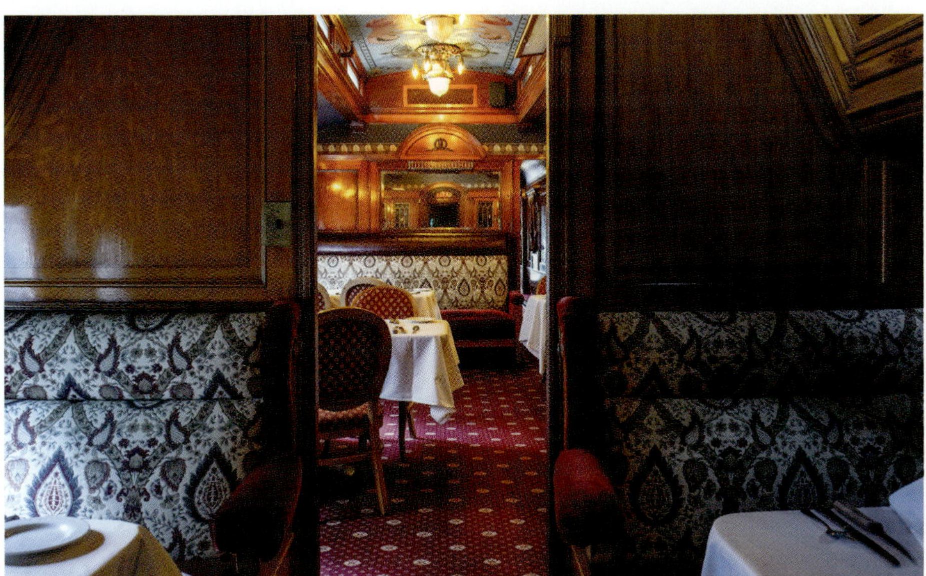

Restored Parlour Car, The Madison Hotel, Morristown, New Jersey

the fact they were willing to accept less money than whites. Railroads also used local foods as a way to generate some savings, but even so, most dining cars were not a money-making venture. However, they were a beloved feature for Gilded Age businessmen and other travelers and a marketing differentiator as competition among the growing number of rail lines heated up. As a result, fine dining thrived on the rails during this era.

Cooking Inside the Pullman Car

How were Pullman Dining Car chefs able to cook such elaborate meals in such a tight space? Everything was organized to maximize space to help accomplish this challenging feat. The cooking area featured a range, broiler, hot water tank, and fuel closet with fire boxes underneath and warming shelves above. The range was connected to a chimney by a stovepipe through the dining car roof. Ample kitchen storage space was allocated to store the coal and charcoal used as fuel. By the late 1890s, the kitchen was powered by compressed gas—the range was uniquely designed so that when a pan or kettle was lifted off the burner, the gas going to that particular burner was shut off completely.

Restored Parlour Car, The Madison Hotel, Morristown, New Jersey

Boston Brown Bread

Boston brown bread has its origins in the hearty wheat, corn, and rye loaves eaten by the Pilgrims and early American colonists in the New England area. These less refined flours were much more attainable than white flour at the time. Even when white flour became more available, Americans retained a nostalgia for Boston brown bread, and it was often featured as an accompaniment in hotels, fine-dining establishments, and dinner party menus during the Gilded Age, sometimes as petite bread and butter sandwiches. It was also a popular breakfast menu choice on Pullman Dining Cars, served alongside other breads such as French loaf, corn bread, hot rolls, and toast.

SERVES 10–12

1 cup cornmeal
1 cup whole wheat flour
1 teaspoon baking soda
1 cup graham flour
1 cup buttermilk
½ cup molasses
1 cup raisins

If baking the bread, preheat oven to 325°F. If steaming the bread, no need to preheat the oven.

Grease an 8 x 5-inch loaf pan and set aside.

In a large bowl, sift together cornmeal, whole wheat flour, and baking soda. Stir in graham flour.

In a medium bowl, mix buttermilk, molasses, and raisins. Add to dry ingredients, stirring until just incorporated. Spoon the batter into the loaf pan and cover with aluminum foil.

To bake the bread, place the pan in the oven and bake for 1 hour, then remove the foil and bake for another 10 minutes. It is done when a toothpick inserted into the center comes out clean. Let the bread cool for 10–15 minutes on a wire rack before removing it from the pan to cool completely.

To steam the bread, place a steamer insert or some crumbled aluminum foil in the bottom of a deep stockpot, then place the pan on top so that it is not touching the bottom. Fill the pot with enough water so that it is two-thirds up the sides. Bring it to a boil, then lower it to a simmer, placing the lid on top. Steam for about 2 hours, adding water if necessary. The bread is done when a toothpick inserted into the center comes out clean.

You can also steam the bread in a crock pot. Add water to cover the bottom of the crock pot, then place the pan inside and close the lid. Steam for 2–3 hours on high. The bread is done when a toothpick inserted into the center comes out clean.

Potage Purée

Adapted from the nineteenth-century cookbook What to Eat, and How to Cook It, *this comforting puréed vegetable soup is a versatile recipe, similar to the Purée of Split Pea featured on an 1897 Pullman vestibuled train dinner menu. Feel free to change it up depending on what is in season or what you have on hand, as railroad chefs did during the Gilded Age.*

SERVES 4

1 tablespoon unsalted butter
1 cup chopped leeks
2 cups chopped white onions
2 cups chopped carrots
2 cups chopped celery
⅛ teaspoon ground cloves
1 teaspoon salt
½ teaspoon white pepper
1 teaspoon dried thyme
1 cup dried lentils or split peas
6 cups vegetable broth

Heat butter in a large heavy-bottomed pot over medium-high heat. Add leeks, onions, carrots, and celery and sauté for 2–3 minutes until just starting to brown.

Add cloves, salt, white pepper, thyme, lentils, and broth and bring to a boil. Turn heat to low, cover pot, and simmer for 2 hours until vegetables are soft.

Remove from heat. Purée soup with a stick blender or place in a blender in batches and blend to desired consistency. Add more vegetable broth to thin if too thick. Pour into bowls and serve.

Spinach à la Crème

Spinach was a common accompaniment to the various meat and game dishes served on Pullman Dining Cars. During the Gilded Age, it was often bathed in a rich cream sauce. As described by Chef Jessup Whitehead in The Steward's Handbook and Guide to Party Catering *(1889), "Spinach, to be truly enjoyed, should never be eaten without liberal saturation of gravy; and French epicures say, 'do not forget the nutmeg.'" This recipe features both. Pullman chefs were smartly following preference and tradition.*

SERVES 4

FOR THE SPINACH:

10 cups packed fresh spinach leaves

½ teaspoon salt

4 cups water

FOR THE CREAM SAUCE:

1 tablespoon unsalted butter

2 tablespoons all-purpose flour

2 cups milk

¼ teaspoon salt

⅛ teaspoon pepper

⅛ teaspoon ground nutmeg

Wash and drain spinach. Remove any tough stems.

Place spinach, salt, and water in a large stockpot. Cover and bring to a boil. Cook for 3–5 minutes until wilted.

Remove the spinach from heat, drain in a colander, and rinse in cold water. Squeeze out all the liquid by pressing down with a wooden spoon or paper towel. Place on a large cutting board and chop into fine pieces. Set aside.

Make the cream sauce by melting the butter in a medium saucepan over medium heat. Add the flour and whisk until it forms a paste. Pour in the milk and cook until thickened, about 3–5 minutes, stirring constantly. Remove from heat and add salt, pepper, and nutmeg.

Add the spinach and stir until incorporated. Place in a serving dish and serve immediately.

Broiled Steak

Broiled beefsteak was a common offering on Pullman Dining Cars, served for breakfast, lunch, and dinner. The most popular cuts included tenderloin, porterhouse, and sirloin, with porterhouse generally considered the best, and sirloin a close second. On an 1882 rail journey from New York to Baltimore, author George Augustus Sala selected fried oysters and beefsteak for his dinner, describing the steak as "well broiled, tender and juicy." It was served with "fried potatoes, crisp and hot, good white bread and excellent lager beer, sparkling, exhilarating and non-intoxicating." This recipe is simplicity at its finest, allowing the flavor of the meat to shine through. Although it calls for broiling the steak as per the Gilded Age preference, grilling is another option for modern palates.

SERVES 4

1 (1½–2 pound) boneless tenderloin, sirloin, or porterhouse steak

½ stick (4 tablespoons) unsalted butter, melted

½ teaspoon seasoned salt

¼ teaspoon black pepper

Parsley sprigs, for garnish

Position the oven rack so that it is about 4 to 5 inches from the broiler. Preheat the broiler to high. Trim the fat from the edge of the steak.

Grease a broiler pan and place the steak on the pan. Broil for 3–5 minutes per side for medium-rare or 6–8 minutes per side for well done.

Remove the steak from the oven and baste with the melted butter. Season with salt and pepper. Cover loosely with aluminum foil and allow to rest for 5–10 minutes. Cut into slices and garnish with parsley.

TEMPERATURE GUIDE

Rare (cool red center): 125°F

Medium-rare (warm red center): 135°F

Medium (warm pink center): 145°F

Medium-well (light pink center): 150°F

Well done (cooked entirely through): 160°F

Blueberry Cake

Fresh blueberries would have been available to Pullman Dining Car chefs in the summer, particularly rail lines that made stops in New England, New Jersey, and Michigan—all areas with a large blueberry presence. Similar to a coffee cake with its streusel topping, this cake could have been served for breakfast or lunch, or even as a snack on one of Pullman's innovative buffet cars, introduced in 1883 to give passengers access to light snacks when the dining car was closed. This was another lucrative concept conceived by Pullman that really took off, with many travelers embracing the idea of lighter meals.

SERVES 8–10

FOR THE CAKE:

½ stick (4 tablespoons) unsalted butter, softened

¾ cup sugar

1 large egg

½ cup milk

2 cups all-purpose flour

2 teaspoons baking powder

½ teaspoon salt

2 cups fresh blueberries

FOR THE STREUSEL TOPPING:

⅓ cup all-purpose flour

½ cup sugar

½ stick (4 tablespoons) cold unsalted butter

2 teaspoons ground cinnamon

Preheat oven to 350°F. Grease a 9-inch round or square cake pan. Set aside.

Place butter, sugar, egg, and milk in a large mixing bowl. Beat on medium-high until well blended.

In a separate bowl, sift flour, baking powder, and salt together. Add to the butter and sugar mixture and stir until just blended (batter will be rather stiff). Gently fold in blueberries. Pour into cake pan.

To make the streusel topping, place flour, sugar, butter, and cinnamon in a deep bowl. Combine using a pastry blender or two knives until small crumbles form. Sprinkle over cake batter.

Place pan in the oven on the center rack and bake for 45 minutes. Let cool on a wire rack. When cool, run a knife around the edge and carefully remove to a plate.

Kitchen, Ebenezer Maxwell Mansion, Philadelphia, Pennsylvania

COOKING SCHOOLS / FOOD DEMOS

Cooking schools were not always a pathway to a restaurant or food industry career as they are today. In the early and mid-nineteenth century, cooking schools were designed to teach upper-class young ladies how to put together elegant meals for fancy dinner parties—especially rich pastries and desserts. Most of the time, these young students were not there by choice, but rather "required" to attend by their mothers.

By the Gilded Age era, this model began to evolve and expand, starting with a charismatic French chef named Pierre Blot, who arrived in New York in 1855. His timing was perfect. Restaurants featuring French food such as Delmonico's were increasing in popularity, and society women often paid French chefs to work as their personal chefs. But other New York residents complained their servants couldn't cook the type of food they desired, particularly the French cuisine that was all the rage. Since there was no formal cooking school in New York that taught this type of cooking, Blot knew if he could establish organized classes for ladies and servants, they could learn French culinary techniques and be entertained at the same time. Seizing on this opportunity, he launched the New York Cooking Academy in 1865. Designating himself "Professor of

The "Servant Issue" during the Gilded Age

As the number of upper- and middle-class families increased during the Gilded Age, more and more families required housekeepers to cook and perform other domestic duties, especially in New York City. However, the lack of good servants continued to pose difficulties, as many were unable to prepare the food their employers desired. These women were often of Irish descent, having arrived in America during the 1840s to escape the potato famine. But since the country they left behind was so devastated by the food shortage there, many never learned how to cook properly and/or were unfamiliar with American-style foods. In addition, most of these young women had been raised in households where they received absolutely zero experience with newfangled appliances such as the cookstove.

Kitchen, Ebenezer Maxwell Mansion, Philadelphia, Pennsylvania

Employers complained about domestics who had no knowledge of lighting and managing a stove, resulting in meals that were late arriving on the table or burned to a crisp. As a result, many meals produced by servants were flavorless and plain, and perhaps even unpalatable at times. So it is not at all surprising that New Yorkers welcomed the "cooking reform" introduced by Pierre Blot with open arms. Professor Blot's game plan was to teach cooking to ladies "of means" as well as their servants, claiming his dishes were not only better than American preparations, but much healthier and more economical too. He wisely addressed the needs of both undertrained servants and unhappy housewives at the same time.

Cooking School, Sloyd Building COURTESY OF THE HISTORICAL SOCIETY OF OLD YARMOUTH, YARMOUTH PORT, MASSACHUSETTS

Gastronomy," he was determined to improve American cooking, using the school as an opportunity to share his ideals.

Of the sixty-two pupils who signed up for his initial classes, many were married ladies from New York's most distinguished and wealthy families. Soon after, he expanded to three classes—two for society "ladies" and one for servants—kicking off a cooking school trend that was widespread throughout the Gilded Age. Blot's simple, instructive manner was a revelation for these students, giving them "a complete insight into the mysteries and economies of the cuisine a la Francais," enthused the *New York Times*.

The public was fascinated and intrigued by Blot's methods. They wanted to see more of him, but in the days before television, the Internet, and social media, opportunities were limited. So in a very ingenious move, he decided to take his cooking classes on the road, traveling first to Boston and later throughout the country. An innovative trailblazer, Blot was essentially America's first "celebrity chef."

The success of Blot's Cooking Academy started a cooking school revolution. His lectures and philosophies "to improve the home table" caught the eye of Margaret Vanderbilt Shepard, granddaughter of railroad and shipping magnate Cornelius Vanderbilt, inspiring her to help establish cooking classes

Maria Parloa—Teaching the Basics

In 1882, Maria Parloa opened a cooking school in New York to teach ladies of all ages and backgrounds. Classes included private lessons as well as free cooking courses for immigrant women during the evening. By 1887, however, she decided to close the school and spend the following year on the lecture circuit. It was a major disappointment to her that women would not attend her classes to make bread, but that they insisted on learning fancy dishes, which she felt were far less important to learn. "Men buy cookbooks for their wives in order that they may learn how to make cake and candy," she said. "I don't teach these and am trying to forget all I know about them."

Gilded Age Heiresses Go to Cooking School

In New York, Gilded Age debutantes and young married women often took classes at the same New York Cooking School location as women who were from the tenements—the United Charities building on 22nd Street and Fourth Avenue. But the similarities typically stopped here. The wealthy girls took their classes during the day, whereas the working women attended in the evenings, after their workday was done. For the affluent, it was simply a way to pass the time. Not wanting to get their hands dirty, many wore dainty silk or satin dresses and left their bonnets on during the lessons. Others showed a genuine interest in cooking, including Margaret Vanderbilt Shepard's daughter Edith, who was said to have "mastered the art of cooking everything from a soft-boiled egg to the most charming dish served by a Sherry or a Delmonico." Emily Vanderbilt Sloane, granddaughter of William H. Vanderbilt, also attended New York Cooking School classes and was said to have been "an apt pupil," even giving pointers to society club chefs.

Philanthropic Support for Cooking Schools

Margaret Vanderbilt Shepard was not the only Vanderbilt to contribute funds toward cooking classes. When Edith Vanderbilt Sloane got married in 1899, she pledged to match her wedding expenses dollar for dollar and put them toward philanthropic causes, including a New York Cooking School course she supported. Charitable fairs were another way the well-to-do showed support for cooking programs. In December 1887, a Doll's Reception was held in the ballroom of Delmonico's to raise money for the New York Cooking School so that the wives of workingmen could attend free of charge. It was so successful that all the dolls were purchased in just three hours. Society women who attended the fair included Caroline Astor, Anna Roosevelt, Margaret Vanderbilt Shepard, Mary Goelet, and Alice Vanderbilt. Many of these women continued to fund and support the New York Cooking School, paying personal visits to ensure all was running smoothly.

in New York as part of the Y.W.C.A., appointing Blot protégé Miss Juliet Corson as an instructor. Miss Corson went on to establish the New York Cooking School in 1873.

Blot's influence also paved the way for a variety of cooking instruction models, including public cooking lectures and demonstrations made popular by his "road show" appearances. Sarah Tyson Rorer, a well-known Philadelphia cooking instructor from the late 1870s through the early twentieth century, gave lectures to packed auditoriums of up to five thousand people. Maria Parloa did the same in the New

Cooking Classes for Men

As Pierre Blot's cooking classes gained in popularity in the late 1860s, he began to receive letters from gentlemen asking if he would host a men's class. So, he added cooking classes for men to his course roster, held in the evenings to accommodate the working schedules of businessmen. Many may have been bachelors who resided in boardinghouses, where the cuisine was often inedible. Others may have wanted the ability to instruct their housekeepers on proper French cooking methods.

England area. Decades before television cooking shows, these culinary authorities were providing cooking as a form of entertainment, and the Gilded Age public ate it up.

Gilded Age Entertainment— Mrs. Rorer at the 1893 World's Fair

World's Fairs began in the mid-nineteenth century as a way to showcase cultures and new technologies from around the world. Each fair highlighted foods in a big way, and Philadelphia Cooking School principal Sarah Tyson Rorer took advantage of this at the Chicago World's Fair in 1893, giving free daily cooking demonstrations. Located inside the Illinois Room in the Woman's Building, her model kitchen was appointed with all the modern conveniences of the day, including "bottles of prepared food and tables on which are all sorts of kitchen utensils." It was situated on a raised platform so attendees (who were both men and women) could see every detail of her work.

Van Duzer's Fruit Extracts, 1886.
LIBRARY OF CONGRESS

Mrs. Rorer taught basic cooking techniques such as how to beat eggs and measure ingredients properly while whipping up a batch of snowy-white cornstarch pudding, giving out samples when she was done. This instruction was peppered with sensational statements meant to shock and horrify her audience, not unlike the reality TV cooking shows of today. Typically, they were warnings about inferior ingredients such as flavor extracts, which she claimed often contained coal tar or rancid butter, with "only four—almond, orange, lemon and vanilla—being what they purport to be." Her lectures were so well attended that she soon became a household name, traveling the country to demonstrate cooking techniques to one packed auditorium after another.

Kitchen, Ebenezer Maxwell Mansion, Philadelphia, Pennsylvania

Roast Chicken, au Jus

*Roast Chicken, au Jus was one of the dishes taught by Pierre Blot at his New York Cooking Academy. (*Au jus *is essentially a meat dish dressed with its own juices or gravy.) Professor Blot explained that the buttered parchment paper prevented the oven's intense heat from scorching the meat and helped catch and hold the steam that rose from the bottom pan, ensuring that it was continually basted and cooked "beautifully almost without care." Although this recipe dates back to 1868, it is easily modified for modern kitchens. Adding a little water to the pan steams the chicken at first, creating a moist interior. Removing the foil or lid toward the end of the cooking time makes the outside of the chicken crispy and turn a nice caramel color.*

SERVES 4

1 large lemon

1 (3–5 pound) chicken

Salt and pepper to taste

1 stick (½ cup) unsalted butter

Preheat oven to 400°F. Grease a roasting pan with a rack.

Cut the lemon in half and squeeze the juice from one half. Season the chicken inside and out with salt, pepper, and lemon juice. Add the remaining lemon half and half of the stick of butter to the cavity. Rub generously with the remaining butter and place on the rack inside the roasting pan.

Wrap a buttered piece of parchment paper or aluminum foil around the chicken (or use a roasting pan with a lid). Add ½ cup of water to the pan.

Bake for 45 minutes and then remove the foil or lid and continue baking until juices run clear and a meat thermometer inserted into the thickest part of the breast and thigh reads 165°F, about 30–45 minutes depending on the size of the chicken.

Remove the chicken from the oven and place on a large cutting board. Let rest for 15 minutes before carving. Skim any surface fat from the juices left in the pan and pour the juices into a pitcher. Bring the juice to the table to serve with the chicken.

Simply Scallops

Delicate and buttery with a tinge of salty brininess, it's hard to imagine that scallops were one of the least consumed shellfish throughout most of the nineteenth century. The lack of scallop offerings was not due to cost—it was simply because they were not as favored. According to Boston Cooking School instructor Maria Parloa, this was due to their "peculiarly sweet flavor." Regardless of this viewpoint, tastes began to change by the 1870s, when demand for this delicacy began to increase in New York markets, particularly in the fall, at the height of the scallop harvesting season. This recipe is adapted from one featured in Pierre Blot's Hand-Book of Practical Cookery. *Although Blot recommends blanching the scallops first, I feel this is an unnecessary amount of cooking for these tender morsels, so I skip this step.*

SERVES 4

1 pound dry sea scallops (see note below)

1–2 tablespoons unsalted butter

Salt and pepper to taste

1–2 tablespoons chopped fresh parsley

Place scallops in a colander and pat dry with paper towels.

Melt butter in a large cast-iron skillet over very high heat. When pan is sizzling, add scallops and spread out.

Cook 2 minutes per side or until opaque, then remove to a platter and sprinkle with salt, pepper, and parsley.

NOTE: *Make sure to get dry scallops for this recipe; wet scallops are treated with a solution of water and sodium tripolyphosphate (STPP) as a preservative, which gives them a spongy texture and imparts a soapy taste. Because they aren't wet and soggy, dry scallops are perfect for searing, which is what you'll be doing here.*

Crispy Potatoes à la Parisienne

Also called Parisienne potatoes, this dish was fashionable throughout the Gilded Age, often served alongside filet of beef, beefsteak, chops, or game, or even as a part of Christmas dinner. New York Cooking School founder Juliet Corson featured it as part of the "Fourth Lesson of the Ladies' Course" in her 1883 Cooking School Text Book. *The round shape makes for a pretty presentation, but you could also cut the potatoes into 1-inch squares or slices, as Sarah Tyson Rorer suggests in an 1887 issue of* Table Talk *magazine.*

SERVES 4

3 pounds waxy potatoes (like Yukon Gold)

½ teaspoon salt, plus ¾ teaspoon

3 tablespoons unsalted butter

3 tablespoons vegetable or canola oil

¼ cup fresh minced parsley

Preheat oven to 425°F.

Wash and peel the potatoes. Use a vegetable scoop or melon baller to cut ball-shaped pieces out of each potato about 1 inch in diameter and place them in a large stockpot of water. (The remaining potato pieces can be placed in a container of cold water to prevent browning and used later to make mashed potatoes or add to soup.)

Add ½ teaspoon salt to the stockpot and bring to a boil. Cook for 5 minutes. Drain in a colander and set aside.

Place the butter and oil in a large cast-iron skillet over medium heat. Once the butter is melted, remove from heat and add potatoes, turning them gently so they are coated on all sides. Sprinkle with ¾ teaspoon salt.

Place the skillet on the center rack of the oven and cook for 15 minutes. Remove the pan from the oven and turn the potatoes so that they can brown on the other side. Return to the oven and cook for an additional 10–15 minutes.

Remove the potatoes from the oven and transfer to a large serving bowl or platter. Sprinkle with parsley and serve.

Cream Puffs

Cream puffs were a popular dessert and tea-time treat during the Gilded Age. Light and airy like a popover, cream puffs are made from a French type of dough called choux paste, which is very different from other types of pastry such as sturdy piecrust and flaky puff paste. It is made by adding butter to boiling water and then adding flour and beaten eggs, which cause the puffs to rise, creating a crispy shell that is hollow on the inside, perfect for filling with whipped cream, custard, or jam. This recipe is adapted from Sarah Tyson Rorer, who described cream puffs as being "very heavy when they get into the oven and very light when they come out."

SERVES 10–12

FOR THE CUSTARD FILLING:

2 cups milk

2 large eggs

1 cup sugar

¾ cup all-purpose flour

Heat the milk in a large heavy pot over medium-high until almost boiling. Turn the heat down to medium and add the eggs, one at a time, beating continuously to prevent curdling. When well mixed, add sugar and flour. Cook gently for 2–3 minutes and then remove from heat. Allow to cool and then refrigerate until needed.

FOR THE CREAM PUFF SHELL:

1 cup water

1 stick (½ cup) salted butter

1 cup all-purpose flour

4 large eggs

Confectioners' sugar for sprinkling (optional)

Preheat oven to 450°F.

Place water in a heavy pot with deep sides and bring to a boil. Carefully add butter to the boiling water, stirring to melt the butter. Add flour and stir dough continuously until it is smooth and forms a soft ball.

Cream Puffs

Cool mixture for 10 minutes and then add the eggs, one at a time, beating after each addition until smooth. Drop mounds of batter onto parchment paper–lined baking sheets with a tablespoon.

Bake at 450° for 15 minutes, then turn oven down to 325°F and bake for 25 additional minutes. (Do not be tempted to open the oven door during the baking process or the puffs may not rise correctly!) They should be nicely browned on the outside. Transfer to a wire rack to cool.

Once cool, split each puff in half with a knife and spoon some custard filling inside, replacing top portion. Sprinkle some confectioners' sugar on top if desired.

Kitchen, Ebenezer Maxwell Mansion, Philadelphia, Pennsylvania

KITCHEN INNOVATIONS

Many ingredients and kitchen conveniences that we take for granted today were either invented or became popular during the Gilded Age, a time of significant technological advances and innovation. For example, chocolate is now such a staple treat in our culture that it is hard to imagine a time when chocolate desserts such as cookies, cake, and ice cream weren't so common or available. But it wasn't until the latter part of the nineteenth century that chocolate confections really started appearing in cookbooks.

Prior to this time, chocolate was consumed mainly as a beverage, often as an alternative to tea or coffee. Hot chocolate was particularly popular during the Gilded Age. Intricate, ornate pitchers designed specifically for serving hot chocolate became very fashionable during the 1880s and 1890s, and porcelain figures depicting the making or serving of hot chocolate were popular parlor and chamber ornaments.

There were some chocolate desserts, in the form of blancmanges, mousse, creams, cream pies, custards, puddings, soufflés, and syrups, but it wasn't

Kitchen, Ebenezer Maxwell Mansion, Philadelphia, Pennsylvania

until improvements in cocoa processing created a much smoother, more delicious-tasting chocolate that chocolate baked goods really took off. In 1828 a Dutchman by the name of van Houten patented a way to simplify cacao processing by pressing out most of the fat and alkalizing the dry cocoa that remained. This revolutionized the manufacturing of chocolate, allowing it to assume solid, liquid, and powdered form, paving the way for all kinds of chocolate dessert possibilities. In the decades that followed, recipes for chocolate cookies, cakes, ice cream, and candies began appearing more frequently in period cookbooks.

An important kitchen convenience introduced during the Gilded Age was the rotary eggbeater, first patented in 1856. By the 1880s, there were many different types of eggbeaters on the market, with new design tweaks launched constantly, such as a side-mounted gear wheel that rotated wire wings to beat the eggs more efficiently, a wire whip, and a spiral eggbeater. All of these would have been a revelation to cooks who previously had to beat eggs by hand, a

Interactive Food Marketing in the Gilded Age

Organized by major food companies, the traveling food expositions that toured the United States in the 1890s were designed to be both entertaining and informative. It was a way to communicate and interact with the public in the days before radio and television. With a combination of elaborate, well-stocked booths and nonstop food demos, these "pure food fairs" attracted big crowds. By promoting and demonstrating their products, these companies also hoped to alleviate concerns about food adulteration scandals that were common at the time, such as cream of tartar cut with rice flour to make it stretch further.

tedious and tiring process that could take an hour or more and was often delegated to a servant.

This new kitchen gadget got a promotional boost from cooking school instructors who started using them in their classes. For example, when Juliet Corson taught her students how to make sponge cake in her Plain Cooks Course in 1881, she could beat the eggs just a few minutes at a time, a much more effective instruction method.

The concept of introducing new innovations to the public quickly took off. Food demonstrations held by cooking experts such as Sarah Tyson Rorer and Maria Parloa were touted as "pure food fairs" by major food manufacturers as a way of advertising their products

Royal Baking Powder, 1897 LIBRARY OF CONGRESS

Hot Chocolate vs. Hot Cocoa

Although we often use the terms *hot chocolate* and *hot cocoa* interchangeably today, during the Gilded Age they were actually two distinctly different beverages. Hot chocolate was thicker and almost syrupy—made from grating fine-quality chocolate and pouring it over boiling water to dissolve. Then fresh milk, egg yolks, and sugar were added. This intense and stimulating drink was so widespread during the era that tea parties would feature a tea service at one end of the table and a chocolate service at the other. Hot cocoa was lighter in color and intensity, made from grated cocoa beans boiled with milk and water, without the addition of eggs and sugar. Period cookbooks often recommended it to soothe those who were ill. In fact, Boston Cooking School instructor Fannie Farmer called cocoa a "nutriment as well as a stimulant," and endorsed its use as a beverage for children.

Baker's Chocolate Ad, circa 1870–1900 BOSTON PUBLIC LIBRARY

and indoctrinating American housewives to modern ingredients meant to make baking and cooking easier, such as baking powder, baking chocolate, and canned foods.

By the late nineteenth century, food ingredient companies had fully realized the power of mass media marketing and started to promote their products via recipes and cookbooks. For example, both Maria Parloa and *Boston Cooking School Magazine* founder Janet McKenzie Hill helped expand the popularity of chocolate desserts by partnering with Baker's Chocolate to publish several recipe pamphlets.

Although introduced in the early part of the nineteenth century, the availability of canned goods such as soups, fruits, vegetables, milk, seafood, and meats really grew in the Gilded Age due to advancements such as the pressure cooker and factory processing. In addition, the expanding rail network and faster steamships allowed these goods to travel to all parts of the United States. Foods like oysters and deviled crab, formerly only available in coastal regions, could now make their way to Midwest cities like Kansas City. And exotic fruits such as grapefruit and pineapple that were formerly inaccessible were now feasible for middle-class families, adding novelty and variety to their diets.

Trade card depicting jars of meat, circa 1876–1890
NEW YORK PUBLIC LIBRARY

Chocolate Macaroons

This popular cookie has had several iterations throughout its history. The version below was adapted from a Pierre Blot recipe featured in a promotional pamphlet published by the Baker's Chocolate company in 1886 called Cocoa and Chocolate: A Short History of Their Production and Use. *Instead of using crushed almonds to make these macaroons, Blot makes a paste out of baking chocolate, sugar, and egg whites. Just these three ingredients yield a deliciously chewy cookie with a crispy exterior that is quick and easy to assemble.*

4 ounces (1 package) unsweetened baking chocolate
3 egg whites
3½ cups confectioners' sugar

Preheat oven to 375°F.

Melt the chocolate in a large glass bowl in the microwave in 30-second increments, stirring well in between. Allow to cool for about 5 minutes.

Mix the egg whites with the chocolate and then sift in the confectioners' sugar a little at a time until it forms a stiff dough.

Using a cookie scoop or teaspoon, scoop balls of dough on cookie sheets lined with parchment paper, leaving about an inch in between.

Bake 10–12 minutes until nicely puffed and then allow to cool on baking sheets before transferring to a wire rack. Cookies will deflate and become flat once they cool.

Dolly Varden Cake

Tall layer cakes were all the rage during the Gilded Age, made light and airy with the newly introduced ingredient called baking powder. One of the most popular was the Dolly Varden Cake, named for the flirty, carefree young woman with colorful clothing and a broad-brimmed hat introduced in Charles Dickens's 1841 book Barnaby Rudge. *Early versions called for three or even four layers of cake in various shades and flavors, meant to mirror Dolly's vibrant dress. Others featured two layers: one was a simple butter cake, sometimes flavored with lemon; the other was made with dried fruits and spices such as raisins, cherries, currants, cloves, cinnamon, and nutmeg. The layers were stacked on top of each other, with a jam, meringue icing, or buttercream frosting sandwiched in between and generously slathered on top. When the cake was cut and placed on a plate, the contrasting layers created a striking effect.*

SERVES 12

3 cups cake flour
2 teaspoons baking powder
2 sticks (1 cup) unsalted butter, softened
2 cups sugar
3 large eggs
1 cup milk
¼ cup molasses
1 cup raisins
1 teaspoon cinnamon
1 teaspoon ground nutmeg
¼ teaspoon ground cloves

Preheat oven to 350°F. Grease and flour two 9-inch round cake pans.

Sift flour and baking powder together, then set aside.

Cream butter and sugar in a large mixing bowl on medium-high. Add eggs one at a time, beating well after each addition. Add flour mixture a little at a time, alternating with the milk until well blended.

Divide the batter in half. Add the remaining ingredients (molasses, raisins, cinnamon, nutmeg, and cloves) to one half, stirring until the ingredients are well mixed.

Pour the white batter into one of the cake pans and the spiced batter into the other. Bake for 35–40 minutes or until a toothpick inserted into the center comes out clean. Cool on a wire rack for about 10 minutes, then loosen from the pans by running a sharp knife or spatula around the edges and inverting on wire racks to cool completely.

Dolly Varden Cake

While the cake is cooling, make the icing. To assemble the cake, place the white layer on the bottom and spread with icing. Top with the spice layer and frost top and sides.

VANILLA BOILED ICING

2 egg whites

1⅓ cups granulated sugar

⅓ cup water

½ teaspoon vanilla

Using an electric mixer, beat the egg whites in a large glass or stainless steel bowl on high speed until soft peaks form, about 3–4 minutes. Set aside.

Make a syrup by combining the sugar and water in a heavy-bottomed pot. Bring to a boil and boil for 5 minutes without stirring.

Pour the syrup over the beaten whites in a thin stream while beating constantly. Add the vanilla and continue beating until very stiff and a spreadable consistency, about 10–15 minutes.

Lemon Meringue Pie

Lemon meringue pie has its origins in a rich lemon pudding that was a signature creation of Mrs. Elizabeth Goodfellow, a nineteenth-century pastry shop proprietress who ran one of the very first cooking schools in America. At some point she cleverly thought to top her famous pudding with fluffy meringue. This sweet blend of stiffly beaten egg whites and sugar would have been much quicker and easier to make once the rotary eggbeater came on the scene. As a result, meringue-frosted puddings and pies were a common and very popular dessert option by the Gilded Age.

SERVES 8–10

FOR THE PIECRUST:

1¼ cup all-purpose flour

½ teaspoon salt

1 stick (½ cup) cold unsalted butter

4 tablespoons cold water

Sift together the flour and salt in a large mixing bowl. Cut in half of the butter with a pastry blender or two knives until evenly mixed and the consistency of coarse sand. Cut in the remaining butter and blend until the dough is in pea-sized pieces.

Add the water a little at a time, stirring lightly with a fork. Use only as much water as you need to make the dough hold together. Form the dough into a circle about an inch thick and wrap in plastic wrap or wax paper. Chill in the refrigerator for 30 minutes.

Place dough on a lightly floured surface and roll into a ⅛-inch thick circle. Place in a 9-inch pie pan and crimp the edges. Line the crust with a piece of parchment paper or aluminum foil and fill the inside with pie weights (either store-bought or dry beans or grains). Chill the crust in the refrigerator for another 30 minutes.

Preheat oven to 375°F.

Remove the crust from the refrigerator and bake for 15 minutes. Remove from the oven and take out the parchment paper and weights. Prick the bottom of the crust all over with a fork. Return the crust to the oven and bake for another 5–10 minutes until golden brown. Cool on a wire rack.

Lemon Meringue Pie

CONTINUED

FOR THE PIE:

2 lemons

½ cup sugar, plus 6 tablespoons

6 large eggs, separated

1 tablespoon all-purpose flour

1 cup cream or milk

Pinch of cream of tartar

Preheat oven to 350°F.

Grate the rinds of both lemons with a microplane or other fine grater. Extract the juice from one lemon and strain through a fine sieve (this should yield ⅓ cup juice). Combine the grated lemon rind and juice with ½ cup sugar, 6 egg yolks, flour, and cream in a large mixing bowl. Stir until thoroughly mixed.

Pour mixture into the prebaked piecrust-lined pan. Cover the edges of the crust with foil to prevent burning. Place on the center rack of the oven and bake for 30 minutes or until firm to the touch.

While the pie is baking, make the meringue by beating 6 egg whites in a large glass or stainless steel bowl with an electric mixer on low until foamy, about 3–4 minutes. Add cream of tartar, increase speed to medium, and continue beating until whites form softly curling peaks. Slowly add 6 tablespoons sugar and keep beating, increasing speed to medium-high, until whites form fluffy, firm peaks that curl slightly at their tips when the beater is raised.

When the pie is done, remove from the oven and spread meringue over the baked pie. Return to the oven and bake for about 10 minutes or until nicely browned on top. Remove and let cool on a wire rack for 1 hour and then refrigerate until ready to serve.

Aunt Lizzie's Pineapple Pie

This recipe is courtesy of my grandfather's Aunt Lizzie, who lived in New York in the early 1900s. Using canned pineapple would have allowed her to quickly put a pie together. Introduced by Dole's Hawaiian Pineapple Company in 1903, canned Hawaiian pineapple was an innovative convenience for cooks throughout the United States. As a result, new recipes that featured the luscious fruit abounded, such as those featured in How We Serve Hawaiian Canned Pineapple, *a little cookbook produced by the Hawaiian Pineapple Packers' Association. A treasure trove of pineapple dishes from the top cooks of the day, such as Fannie Farmer, Sarah Tyson Rorer, and Maria Parloa, it includes several pineapple pie recipes similar to Aunt Lizzie's.*

1 (20-ounce) can crushed pineapple
¼ cup sugar, plus 6 tablespoons
2 tablespoons cornstarch
3 large eggs, separated
2 tablespoons unsalted butter
1 (9-inch) pre-baked pie shell (see page 41)

Preheat oven to 400°F. Open and drain the crushed pineapple, reserving 1 cup of the juice.

In a medium saucepan, bring ¼ cup sugar, cornstarch, reserved juice, and egg yolks to a boil over medium heat. Cook until thickened, about 2 minutes. Add butter and crushed pineapple. When butter is melted and mixture is well combined, set aside to cool slightly.

While pineapple filling is cooling, beat the egg whites in a large glass or stainless steel bowl with an electric mixer on medium speed until soft peaks form, about 3–4 minutes. Slowly add 6 tablespoons sugar and keep beating until whites form fluffy, firm peaks that curl slightly at their tips when the beater is raised.

Pour filling into pie shell. Spread meringue over the filling, covering entire surface to the crust. Bake for 8–12 minutes until meringue is nicely browned.

CHAPTER TWO
OUTDOOR EATS

PICNICS
Roll Sandwiches
Saratoga Chips
Sweet Pickles
Peanut Cookies
Mrs. Rorer's Chocolate Cake

FOURTH OF JULY
Fried Chicken
Dutch Cucumbers
Herbed Tomatoes
Ginger Cookies
Lemon Sherbet

STRAWBERRY FETES AND FESTIVALS
Strawberries and Cream
Strawberry Shortcake

ICE CREAM SOCIALS
Strawberry Ice Cream
Wafers à la Française
French Vanilla Ice Cream

The success or failure of a picnic depends mainly upon a good supply of the right kinds of food and drink. . . . There is no better stimulus for failing appetites than plenty of fresh air.

—*THE NEW ENGLAND KITCHEN MAGAZINE*, 1894

OUTDOOR ACTIVITIES and entertaining were very popular during the Gilded Age. These included ice cream socials, strawberry fetes and festivals, and outings to special picnic spots, such as sailing across a lake or traveling to the beach. As a result, ingenious methods of keeping foods fresh and attractive were devised, such as wrapping items in fancy papers and tying them with string into pretty packages. Gilded Age picnickers even figured out how to bring ice cream along with them. This chapter highlights these outdoor settings, occasions, and leisure activities, featuring foods included in alfresco celebrations.

Gilded Age Picnic

PICNICS

Eating out of doors was not a new concept in the Gilded Age, but outdoor parties and other activities where it was customary to eat a meal of some kind outside became very popular during the era. Nature settings were seen as being particularly attractive for dining and socializing. An 1889 article in *Ingalls Magazine* states that "May is preeminently the month for picnics. Not the opening days—which are apt to be too chilly—but the last of the month, which we may rightly claim, by reason of work accomplished, sunny skies and fragrant woods, and the general demand of the system for relaxation." This author claims that July should be out of the question for picnics, but evidence abounds for Gilded Age summer outings, particularly those near lakes and streams where it was generally cooler. For example, an 1870 diary entry from a Mrs. Almira MacDonald outlines a family excursion in July across Seneca Lake in New York to Johnson's Cove for a picnic.

A typical Gilded Age picnic menu featured dishes such as cold roast chicken, sardines, hard-boiled eggs in beet juice, Boston brown bread and buttered rolls, sweet pickles, plum jelly or orange marmalade, watermelon, peaches, grapes, chocolate loaf cake, and delicate cake (likely some type of sponge cake). Some cookbooks from the era organized picnic menus seasonally, with items reflecting the time of year, such as ham sandwiches, marble cake, and oranges for spring; cold broiled chicken, sliced tomatoes, and lemon ice for summer; and fish chowder, baked apples, and roasted sweet potatoes for fall. Sandwiches could be made on sliced bread or crafted out of split finger rolls, the two sides attractively tied together with a narrow ribbon. And for those occasions deemed extra special, a freezer filled with frozen ice cream would be brought along. In order to carry this frosty treat to the picnic without melting, the freezer would be packed in lots of ice and wrapped in a heavy carpet.

In addition to picnics, the practice of taking an annual

How to Pack a Picnic Basket

An 1891 book called *Dining Room and Kitchen* by Mrs. Grace Townsend is a veritable "picnic how-to" for the era. Mrs. Townsend devotes a whole chapter to "Lunches, Picnics and Parties," outlining various outdoor occasions, how to host them, and the best food for each. Many of the tips she includes are directions we still follow today, whether taking our lunch to the beach or pool, on a picnic, or even to work. She includes suggestions like "when rolls are taken, wrap each two buttered and laid together, in tissue paper" and tongue-in-cheek advice such as "cookies always taste better than rich cakes at a picnic." She also stressed the importance of a properly packed picnic basket. The plates, cups, and sauce dishes were placed in the basket first, gently positioned with the towels and napkins. The food items went in next, tightly and carefully placed on top, then covered with a tablecloth and oil cloth. All of this would be accompanied by lemonade, coffee, and tea, which would require bringing along a coffeepot with prepared coffee tied in a white flannel or muslin bag and a teapot with tea tied in a neat paper package.

Ladies Picnic, Grassy Point, Ontario, 1909 DESERONTO ARCHIVES

summer holiday began to become more common in the Gilded Age. Reduced railway fares made it possible even for those on limited incomes and large families to escape the "close streets and smoky towns" and get some fresh air, through a visit to either the seaside or the country. Railways such as New York's West Shore Railroad Company published books advertising "Picnic and Excursion Parties," inviting travelers to see "some of the delightful spots on the West Shore of the Hudson River for one-day excursions." The train would take them to places such as Barren Island, which had a dance pavilion, merry-go-round, swings, and summer houses; Cole's Grove, featuring shady areas for

Picnic Lemonade

"Always take lemons and sugar or prepare the syrup at home. Take lemons and squeeze them in a glass jar, add sugar, and stir into a thin syrup. Add no water, as that would be extra to carry. Serve by putting a spoonful into each glass of water. Iced tea can be served in the same way."

—MRS. GRACE TOWNSEND, *DINING ROOM AND KITCHEN* (1891)

Horse Racing

Horse racing was a favorite outdoor pastime for the upper classes during the Gilded Age. A popular spot in the New York area was Jerome Park in the Bronx, financed by wealthy racing enthusiasts Leonard Jerome, August Belmont, and William Travers. Launched in 1866, it featured a sprawling clubhouse with excellent meals and a spacious ballroom. Situated on a picturesque, wooded bluff, the clubhouse was open all hours of the day and night and quickly became a key rendezvous for high society.

In 1867 the track was the site of the first Belmont Stakes, the oldest of the three Triple Crown horse racing events. The concept soon moved west, with the first Kentucky Derby held in 1875, inspired by horse races witnessed in Europe by Meriwether Lewis Clark, the grandson of William Clark of the Lewis and Clark expedition. Although the Derby's famous signature cocktail, the mint julep, didn't became its official drink until 1939, it has been enjoyed there since the early years. As per Derby lore, in 1877 Clark toasted Polish actress Helena Modjeska with a generously sized mint julep meant for sharing, but she liked it so much she drank the entire glass and ordered another.

picnicking, a beach, and boating and bathing facilities; and Rockland Lake Park, which had a lake fed by crystal clear springs, boating and fishing docks, and baseball fields.

American East Coast beaches were also popular summer holiday and day trip destinations. New Yorkers flocked to nearby Coney Island, Brighton Beach, and Manhattan Beach, as well as New Jersey beaches such as Sea Girt and Long Branch. Philadelphians favored Atlantic City and Cape May.

Oyster Roasts and Clambakes

Many Gilded Age beach outings featured festive oyster roasts and clambakes. Oyster roasts at the New Jersey shore typically involved building a big bonfire on the beach to roast oysters, clams, fish, and sweet corn, either nestled in the fire or roasted in an iron pan set on the bed of hot coals. Once the oysters opened up, they were placed in a separate pan with some melted butter; seasoned with salt, pepper, and vinegar; and then eaten steaming hot. Others preferred eating them right from the shells.

For a clambake, clams were dug from their hiding places in the wet sand when the tide was out, then baked on hot stones. Boston Cooking School teacher and cookbook author Mary Lincoln recommended selecting a dozen or more large, round stones, piling wood on top, and making a good brisk fire to thoroughly heat them. She advised that the clams should be well rinsed and free of sand and grit, which was typically done right there in the salt water on the beach. The clams would be piled over the stones, then heaped high in the center. Any edibles that were to be steamed with the clams were included here too, such as corn or fish. They were then covered with a thick layer of seaweed and a canvas, blanket, or even leaves placed on top to hold in the steam.

The baking time depended on the size and quantity of the clams. Mrs. Lincoln suggested peeking after about a half hour to see if they opened easily, but warned those in the middle could warrant a longer cooking time to ensure all were baked safely and evenly. She recommended eating the clams right from the shell, piping hot, dipped in melted butter and vinegar, accompanied by other fare such as boiled ham, stuffed bluefish, fresh ears of sweet corn, brown bread, sweet potatoes, baked Indian pudding, watermelon, and molasses cookies.

When the stones are hot enough to crackle as you sprinkle water on them, they are ready. Brush the embers off, letting them fall between and around the stones. Put a thin layer of wet seaweed on the hot stones to keep the lower clams from burning and create enough steam to begin the cooking.

—MARY LINCOLN, BOSTON COOKING SCHOOL TEACHER AND COOKBOOK AUTHOR

AN OYSTER ROAST

In his book *Rambles and Reflections*, Pennsylvania lawyer and judge Thomas Jefferson Clayton writes about an oyster roast experience along the Chesapeake Bay in Virginia in 1892: "We took a stroll over the farm, and on our return enjoyed a grand oyster roast upon the shore at the end of the lawn. The mansion is beautifully situated upon a rising knoll, gently sloping to the water's edge. The Chesapeake Bay at this place is very wide. The shore is very irregular and full of little bays running into the main land from a few hundred yards to many miles. . . . The branches, or little bays, are planted with the most delicious and finely flavored oysters in the world. A great abundance of them were daily provided for our use and wood was always ready for a roast."

Long Branch (New Jersey) Boardwalk, 1897 FLICKR COMMONS

All of these seaside resorts became much more accessible via rail. The cooler Rhode Island shoreline also attracted Gilded Age millionaires from New York, Philadelphia, and even more distant locations such as St. Louis and South Carolina. Flush with money, these barons of industry built expansive mansions in Newport, as well as nearby Narragansett and Conanicut Island, in order to escape the stifling summer heat of the city. Newport was considered "rigidly exclusive" and Narragansett "free and easy." As a result, Newport society belles would often sail across the bay to Narragansett Pier, where they could flirt, dance, bathe in the surf, and eat ice cream under more relaxed conditions.

Easton's Beach, Newport, Rhode Island, 1901 WIKIMEDIA COMMONS

Roll Sandwiches

Gilded Age picnic sandwiches could be made on sliced bread or the roll variety. Crafted out of split finger rolls, these roll sandwiches were filled with minced meat such as ham, cold boiled tongue, or chicken, mixed with a rich homemade mayonnaise made from mashed egg yolks, butter, and cream. The two halves were then tied together with a narrow ribbon. In the article "Provisions for Picnics," featured in an 1893 issue of The Outlook, *Christine Terhune Herrick suggests using different-colored ribbons as an attractive way to indicate the filling type.*

SERVES 8

- 4 cups cooked, finely chopped chicken or ham
- 1 teaspoon salt
- ¼ teaspoon pepper
- 5 hard-boiled egg yolks
- 2 tablespoons unsalted butter, melted
- ½ cup milk
- 8 oblong sandwich or club rolls

In a large bowl, mix the chicken or ham with the salt and pepper. Set aside.

Mash the hard-boiled egg yolks in a medium bowl with the back of a fork until a very fine consistency. Add the melted butter and mix well. Gradually pour in the milk and stir with a whisk until smooth. Add to the bowl with the chopped meat and stir until well coated.

Cut the rolls in half, lengthwise. Scoop out the center portion and fill each with ½ cup of the chicken or ham mixture. Tie the two halves of each roll together with a pretty ribbon. If using multiple fillings, different ribbon colors can be used to indicate sandwich type.

Saratoga Chips

Saratoga chips are the precursor to the potato chips that are now an integral feature on picnic, barbeque, and lunch menus throughout America. We can thank a Saratoga Springs, New York, restaurant called Moon's Lake House for making them popular. The restaurant opened in 1853, and according to legend, in August of that year a fussy customer (some say it was railroad magnate Cornelius Vanderbilt) repeatedly sent his plate of "Moon's Fried Potatoes" back to the kitchen, complaining they were sliced too thick. In frustration, chef George Crum sliced up some potatoes razor-thin, fried them until crisp, and seasoned them with extra salt. The super-thin fried potato style took hold, and by the 1870s recipes for crispy Saratoga chips appeared frequently in American cookbooks.

SERVES 4

3 large Yukon Gold potatoes, washed and peeled
Lard or vegetable oil, for frying
Salt

Slice the potatoes with a mandoline or sharp knife into very thin slices (⅛ inch thick or thinner). The slicing attachment of a food processor works well too. Place the sliced potatoes in a large bowl of ice water for at least 10 minutes. Drain and pat dry with paper towels.

Heat 2 cups of lard or vegetable oil in a large cast-iron or sauté pan over medium-high heat. When shimmering, carefully add 5 or 6 slices of potato. Use long tongs to separate and cook on one side until they are a delicate yellow color, about 3–4 minutes. Turn and brown on the other side, another minute or two. (The hot lard or oil may splatter, so it's best to do this while wearing a kitchen mitt.)

Remove the potato slices with tongs or a slotted spoon and drain on a baking sheet or large tray lined with paper towels. Sprinkle with salt. Continue with the remaining potatoes. Serve warm or room temperature.

To take along to a picnic, Mrs. Grace Townsend recommended, "Saratoga chips look nicest carried in fancy papers which can be thrown away."

—*DINING ROOM AND KITCHEN* (1891).

Sweet Pickles

Pickling is a loose term that refers to vegetables brined and marinated in vinegar. Using the refrigerator method, such as in this recipe, quickens the brining process. Spices, vinegar, and sugar can vary depending on taste preferences. Sweet pickles such as these were often the preferred type for Gilded Age picnics. A Cassel's Family Magazine *from 1888 suggests serving sweet pickles with cold meats or a "piece of bread and butter when your appetite is jaded or cloyed."*

MAKES 7 CUPS

6 cups thinly sliced cucumbers
1 cup thinly sliced onion
1½ cups sugar
1½ cups vinegar
½ teaspoon salt
½ teaspoon mustard seed
½ teaspoon celery seed
½ teaspoon ground turmeric

Place the cucumber and onion slices in a large glass or ceramic bowl, alternating the layers. Set aside.

Combine the sugar, vinegar, salt, mustard seed, celery seed, and turmeric in a medium saucepan over high heat. Bring to a boil, stirring just until the sugar is dissolved.

Remove the brine from the heat and pour over the cucumber and onion mixture. Cool slightly, then cover and refrigerate for at least 24 hours before serving. Store up to one month in the refrigerator.

PEANUT COOKIES

Today most peanut-flavored cookies are made with peanut butter, but this recipe uses chopped peanuts instead, yielding a delightfully crunchy cookie that is not too sweet. Peanut butter was not introduced until the second half of the nineteenth century, and even then, it wasn't as we know it today, as the oil would often separate and oxidize. It was also originally promoted as a health food, marketed to people who frequented health spas. Some people used a special nut butter mill or even a coffee mill to grind peanuts themselves.

MAKES 3½ DOZEN

1 stick (½ cup) unsalted butter, softened
1 cup sugar
1 large egg
¼ cup milk
1¾ cups all-purpose flour
1 teaspoon baking powder
1 cup chopped unsalted peanuts

Preheat oven to 400°F.

Using an electric mixer, cream butter and sugar on medium-high speed until well blended. Mix in the egg and milk.

Sift flour and baking powder together in a separate bowl. Add to wet ingredients and mix until well combined. Stir in peanuts.

Drop teaspoonfuls of dough on baking sheets lined with parchment paper and bake for 10–12 minutes. Cool on a wire rack.

Mrs. Rorer's Chocolate Cake

This recipe is from Philadelphia cooking instructor Sarah Tyson Rorer, adapted from the recipe book of Anna Smith Maxwell of Philadelphia's Ebenezer Maxwell Mansion, a historic fully restored mansion built in 1859. Dubbed the "First Lady of the House," Anna's diary alludes to the fact that she attended some of Mrs. Rorer's cooking classes or lectures in the late 1800s. This cake is extremely versatile and portable, as it contains no icing and can be baked as a loaf—perfect for picnics and other outdoor gatherings.

SERVES 10–12

2 ounces (½ package) unsweetened baking chocolate
1 stick (½ cup) butter, softened
1½ cups sugar
4 large eggs, separated
½ cup milk
1¾ cups all-purpose flour
1 teaspoon vanilla extract
1 teaspoon baking powder
Confectioners' sugar for sprinkling (optional)

Preheat oven to 350°F. Grease and flour a 9-inch springform or 9 x 5-inch loaf pan. Set aside.

Place the chocolate in a microwave-safe dish and heat in the microwave on high for 1 minute. Take out the dish and give the chocolate a stir. Continue doing this in 30-second intervals until chocolate is melted. Set aside.

Using an electric mixer, beat the butter in a large bowl on medium-high speed until creamy. Gradually add the sugar, then the egg yolks. Turn down to low and add the milk, then the melted chocolate and flour. Mix until well incorporated.

In a separate bowl, beat the whites of the eggs until firm peaks form, about 6–7 minutes. Add to the chocolate mixture, stirring until well blended. Stir in the vanilla and baking powder until just combined.

Pour the batter into a springform or loaf pan. Bake for 35–45 minutes if using a springform pan and 55–60 minutes if using a loaf pan, or until a toothpick inserted into the top comes out clean. Place pan on a wire rack to cool, about 30 minutes for the springform pan and 15–20 minutes for the loaf pan, then invert on the wire rack to cool completely. Just before serving, sprinkle with confectioners' sugar if desired.

Gilded Age Fourth of July Picnic

FOURTH OF JULY

Fourth of July celebrations began appearing in full force during the nineteenth century. Era periodicals such as *Godey's Lady's Book* and *Demorest's Family Magazine* contained short stories featuring nostalgic or "old-fashioned" Fourth of July picnics, leading women of the time to re-create this atmosphere for their own families. This included all the things we have come to associate with the holiday today: American flags waving in the hot summer breeze from front porches; village green bandstands decked out in red, white, and blue; bands playing a Sousa march; lawn games; and picnic tables covered with red and blue gingham tablecloths. Picnic fare for the occasion included platters of hearty fried chicken, baked ham, sandwiches, salads, cakes, pies, tarts, dishes of red strawberries and raspberries, strawberry ice cream, lemonade, and ginger beer.

Fourth of July Printed Menus

In the Gilded Age, even stationery companies got into the patriotic spirit by offering Fourth of July–themed menus printed especially for the occasion. In 1885 a Philadelphia company called Longhead & Co. designed a menu printed in old-style lettering with a picture of the Liberty Bell in the center. The other side featured a miniature replica of the Declaration of Independence, including the signatures of its signers. It was devised to be rolled up like a scroll and tied with a bright ribbon.

Independence Day celebrations were much less formal than other Gilded Age holiday meals such as Thanksgiving, Christmas, and New Year's. The rules of etiquette could be slightly relaxed once outside the dining room. However, ladies still had to be mindful that they were dining in public and might be exposed to social criticism. Some items might be off-limits—eating a piece of fried chicken, for example. According to nineteenth-century cookbook author and etiquette authority Eliza Leslie, "No lady looks worse than when gnawing a bone, even of game or poultry. Few *ladies* do it. In fact, nothing should be slurped or gnawed in public; neither corn bitten off the cob, nor melon nibbled from the rind." Miss Leslie was sending this warning to the growing middle class at the time who were working their way up the social ladder.

Fourth of July Picnic, 1885 FLICKR COMMONS

Games were typically reserved for after supper when it was cooler and included "pin the star on the flag." Just like pin the tail on the donkey, each guest was blindfolded and twirled around three times, then instructed to pin a white paper star in its proper position on a large flag hanging from

The DAR and the Fourth of July

The Gilded Age was a time of nostalgia and interest in America's early days. It was also a time when many women were seeking their own independence, with the women's suffrage movement in full swing. But patriotic-minded women felt frustrated, since they were excluded from similar men's groups. So several enterprising women formed their own organization in 1890, the Daughters of the American Revolution (DAR), which is still going strong today. A 1908 *Table Talk* magazine depicts one way this new group celebrated the Fourth of July—with a themed tea, stating there is "no more fitting or charming way of marking Independence Day than by giving a Colonial Tea." Like Fourth of July picnics, it instructed keeping with the red, white, and blue color scheme and featuring a "daintily appointed tea table" with a centerpiece made from a child's drum laced with blue ribbon and garnished with tulle and forget-me-nots. Bonbon boxes in the shape of three-cornered hats filled with candied violets and tiny knapsacks of papier-mâché filled with salted nuts were suggested table souvenirs. The menu included cold sliced ham with apple jelly, hot biscuits with strawberry preserves, oyster patties, chicken salad, cheese wafers, coffee, tea, and tea cakes, all served on "blue china of historic pattern."

the side of the porch. Relay races were another popular activity, as well as the playing of patriotic songs such as "The Star-Spangled Banner" on small horns, whistles, drums, and harmonicas, followed by the town's fireworks display.

An 1898 issue of *American Kitchen Magazine* likened Fourth of July festivities to a garden party: "an old-fashioned, all day celebration, sort of a summer Thanksgiving, with friends and relatives coming from near and far." Although described as an open-house format, most guests preferred to stay outside, sitting on red, white, and blue rugs, hammocks, and cushions scattered around the piazza and lawn. Other decorations included flags and Japanese lanterns—even the croquet wickets and ring-toss games were decorated in patriotic colors. The dinner table was positioned under the shade of a large tree, covered in a long white cloth looped at the corners with flags.

Flower arrangements were scarlet geraniums and blue myrtle, keeping with the patriotic theme. In the middle was a charming fort constructed out of small white frosted cakes, each topped with a miniature flag, which guests pinned on each other after dinner as "badges of loyalty." The china was red and white, and a paper napkin flag was placed next to each place setting, along with a firecracker-shaped box filled with red cinnamon drops, white peppermints, and chocolates wrapped in blue paper.

Fourth of July Dinner Menu, New Gladstone Hotel, Narragansett Pier, Rhode Island, 1899 NEW YORK PUBLIC LIBRARY

The patriotic colors carried over to the main menu, which included snowy white boiled halibut and lobster salad served in its own bright red shell. Roast lamb and jellied chicken were featured alongside mashed potatoes and sliced tomatoes. There were bowls of ruby-hued cherries and currants placed on trays of chipped ice. Desserts included refreshing strawberry sherbet served with the little white cakes. With the coffee, crackers were brought out with a choice of Edam or Neufchatel cheese to nibble on during the fireworks display. And salty peanuts and crisp gingerbread were available to snack on throughout the day, accompanied by thirst-quenching sweet-tart lemonade, a welcome drink in the excessive heat.

Fried Chicken

Gilded Age cookbooks feature many different fried chicken recipe variations. Some are served with gravy or a white sauce or even cooked in cream, as Oscar Tschirky (the head chef at the famed Waldorf-Astoria hotel) directed in The Cook Book *(1896). Some recommend frying the chicken in butter, some in lard. The simple recipe below is based on the "Southern style."*

1 (2½–3 pound) package bone-in chicken pieces
1 teaspoon salt
¼ teaspoon pepper
1 cup all-purpose flour
½ stick (4 tablespoons) unsalted butter

Rinse each piece of chicken under cold water, then set on a large tray or baking sheet and let dry. Sprinkle each piece with salt and pepper. Place the flour in a low dish or bowl (a pie plate works well). Roll each piece of chicken in the flour to cover.

Melt the butter in a large saucepan over medium heat. Add the chicken pieces and fry until internal temperature reaches 165°F and the outside has browned, turning occasionally. Cooking time will vary depending on the size of the pieces. It can be up to 20–25 minutes for the breasts and thighs, whereas drumsticks and wings usually cook in 10–15 minutes. Not all pieces might fit at the same time, depending on the size of the pan, so feel free to cook the larger pieces first.

Cool on a wire rack set over a baking sheet to retain crispness.

Dutch Cucumbers

Cucumber salads and pickles were commonly featured on Gilded Age Fourth of July picnic menus. This tangy salad with a hint of sweetness is a family recipe handed down by my grandmother, Catherine Demarest Ellsworth. She typically served them with Herbed Tomatoes *(see page 73)**. According to cooking school instructor Sarah Tyson Rorer, Dutch Cucumbers were "large cucumbers preserved in brine richly flavored with dill, also called 'Holland pickles.'"*

My grandmother did have Dutch in her background, but I'm not sure if this recipe was really of Dutch origin. The "Dutch" could refer to the type of cucumber—the longer, thinner seedless variety that are often called English cucumbers. Feel free to use any type of cucumber you like. I like to peel them first, as it gives them a pretty, striped look.

SERVES 4–6

2 cups thinly sliced cucumber
1 cup thinly sliced onion
½ cup white wine or cider vinegar
½ cup cold water
¼ cup sugar
¾ teaspoon salt
⅛ teaspoon freshly ground black pepper

Place cucumbers and onions in a deep bowl.

Combine the remaining ingredients in a small bowl and pour over the cucumber and onion slices. Cover and chill several hours or overnight. Drain liquid prior to serving.

Herbed Tomatoes

Bright red tomatoes corresponded with the patriotic color scheme so common in the Gilded Age. Heirloom tomatoes are delicious in this recipe and provide the greatest authenticity, but beefsteak tomatoes work well too.

SERVES 6–8

6 large ripe heirloom or beefsteak tomatoes

⅔ cup salad oil (vegetable, canola, or olive)

¼ cup white wine or cider vinegar

¼ cup chopped parsley

¼ cup sliced scallions

¼ teaspoon freshly ground black pepper

2 teaspoons minced fresh thyme, tarragon, or basil leaves

1 clove garlic, minced

1 teaspoon salt

Cut the tomatoes into wedges and place in a deep bowl.

Combine the remaining ingredients in a jar with a lid to make a dressing. Shake well and pour over the tomatoes. Cover and chill several hours or overnight.

To serve, place Dutch Cucumbers (see page 71) in the center of a large shallow bowl or platter and arrange Herbed Tomatoes artfully around the cucumbers.

Ginger Cookies

This ginger cookie recipe is adapted from Abby Fisher's cookbook, What Mrs. Fisher Knows About Old Southern Cooking. *Published in 1881, it is the oldest known cookbook written by a formerly enslaved person. Born in 1832, Abby grew up in plantation kitchens in South Carolina. There she honed her culinary skills and became a phenomenal cook, which catapulted her to success later in life. Gaining her freedom after the Civil War, she and her husband, Alexander, and eleven children migrated to California in 1877 and set up a pickles and preserves business in San Francisco. Mrs. Fisher won a diploma at the Sacramento State Fair in 1879, its highest award, and two medals in 1880 at the San Francisco Mechanics' Institute Fair. Her ginger cookie recipe is soft, yet crispy at the edges—true perfection and perfect for family gatherings.*

1 stick (½ cup) butter, softened
½ cup sugar
½ cup molasses
2½ cups all-purpose flour
1 teaspoon baking soda
1 tablespoon ground ginger (or to taste)
1 teaspoon cinnamon
1 teaspoon allspice

Preheat oven to 350°F.

Using an electric mixer, cream butter and sugar on medium-high speed. Add molasses.

In a large bowl, sift together flour, baking soda, ginger, cinnamon, and allspice. Add to the butter, sugar, and molasses mixture and mix until ingredients form a soft dough.

Shape dough into a ball, adding flour in small increments if dough seems sticky. Roll out onto a floured board and cut into shapes with a cookie cutter, or scoop dough into walnut-sized balls and roll in granulated sugar.

Place 2 inches apart on baking sheets lined with parchment paper and bake for 10–12 minutes. Cool on a wire rack.

Lemon Sherbet

This refreshing summertime favorite is derived from the Middle Eastern drink called sharab, *a cold, fruity nonalcoholic beverage. Eventually the cooling treat made its way to Europe and then America. By the 1880s, sherbet recipes in the United States had begun to evolve from a beverage to an icy, scoopable dessert. Era cookbooks featured flavors such as pineapple, strawberry, raspberry, currant, lemon, and orange, often with the addition of gelatin or egg whites to give them a lighter, more creamy consistency than fruit water ices. By the early twentieth century, many recipes still incorporated gelatin or egg whites, but some started to substitute milk or cream to give sherbet a smoother texture, similar to the frozen treat we know today.*

1½ cups sugar
4 cups (1 quart) 2% milk
Juice and zest of 2 lemons
Mint sprig for garnish (optional)

Place sugar and milk in a large heavy pot and bring to a boil over medium heat. Remove from heat and let cool in the pot for 10 minutes, then pour into a glass bowl and chill in the refrigerator for 1 hour.

Remove from the refrigerator and add lemon juice and zest. Pour mixture into the chilled bowl of an ice cream maker and mix until frozen as per ice cream maker manufacturer's instructions.

Transfer to a glass bowl and store in the freezer until ready to serve. Scoop into dishes and garnish with a mint sprig if desired.

STRAWBERRY FETES AND FESTIVALS

A favorite Gilded Age summer entertainment on warm June evenings was the community's annual strawberry fete or festival. These were highly anticipated outdoor socials, sponsored by churches, schools, and other organizations as fund-raising events, featuring a copious amount of fresh-picked strawberries with whipped cream, as well as a variety of cakes and pies made with the luscious fruit. Just like today, people welcomed the chance to get together out of doors and mingle in the fresh air after being cooped up inside all winter.

Ornamental strawberries and desserts, Mrs. Beeton's Book of Household Management, *1861* WELLCOME COLLECTION

By the turn of the twentieth century, many communities across the United States had perfected their annual strawberry fete, sometimes referred to as

STRAWBERRY SHORTCAKE

Strawberry shortcake recipes began popping up in American cookbooks in the mid-1800s, likely evolving from shortcake and biscuit-type desserts that had been common in England, such as Derby Short Cakes (also known as Derby Biscuits or Derby Cakes), thick biscuits sweetened with sugar and sometimes currants, cut into scalloped rounds. However, these early biscuits still would have been rather flat since they contained no rising agent. But once chemical leavenings such as pearlash (made from lye) and baking powder came on the scene in the nineteenth century, they were added to shortcake recipes, resulting in full, fluffy biscuits with a softer crumb. Since they are not overly sweet like a cake, they pair perfectly with ripe, seasonal strawberries and whipped cream.

Strawberry-Picking Parties

Strawberry-picking parties became popular in the late 1890s and were often given "to a young girl on the eve of departure for boarding school." Everything was planned out ahead of time to ensure partygoers (and their fancy clothing) were not soiled picking the berries. Large square plots of growing berries were covered in straw so that "there was no grit and the picking was very easy." The hostess, dressed in a frilly white lace dress and hat, would greet each guest with a fancy green basket tied with red ribbons for the berry picking. Lady guests wore similar dresses, and often carried a parasol trimmed with fancy ribbons. Men wore afternoon suits of light flannel cloth. Those who considered themselves "too fine or indolent for such sylvan sport were provided with a plate of fruit." After the picking was over, guests were served petite sandwiches, lobster salad, petits fours, and other "dainties," along with the requisite strawberries and cream, strawberry ice cream, strawberry ice, and strawberry-flavored cakes and confections. It was considered a "both pretty and enjoyable" way to spend an afternoon and evening.

a regale, turning it into an art form. Decorations were just as important as the food, with ladies' magazines instructing women to "secure as many old-fashioned garden flowers, also a profusion of vines, if possible, particularly the strawberry vine, called the potentilla, found in quantities in fields and lanes." These were used to decorate the inside of the house or building where the fete was held, with garlands of vines running from the corners of the room to the chandelier and looped over white curtains. A potted strawberry plant in fruit or flower was placed in the center of each table.

Various outside booths offered items for sale such as flowers, fresh lemonade, and candy. Each booth was decorated to match the items being sold. For example, the flower booth was draped in white cheesecloth, smilax, and roses; the lemonade booth was shaped like a well, with the lemonade served

Strawberries and Politics

Gilded Age society enjoyed hosting strawberry-themed luncheons, teas, and suppers in the spring and summer. This was especially true in Washington, DC. In May 1870, President Ulysses S. Grant's wife, Julia, gave a strawberry lunch party at the White House. Guests included not only the president, but members of his cabinet and their families, as well as generals and their wives, judges, naval captains, and foreign dignitaries. In fact, President Grant moved a cabinet meeting specifically so his cabinet members could attend the festive event. The *Richmond Dispatch* enthused, "The flowers, fruits and berries, together with the gold and silver adornments, rendered the lunch-table a thing beautiful to look upon." Afterward, Julia hosted a formal reception for the guests until 5:00 p.m. A few years later, the *New York Times* reported on a magnificent strawberry party at the Brentwood, "the suburban villa of Capt. Carlisle Patterson, Superintendent of the Coast Survey," for Washington society in 1876.

in dippers from a large bucket; and the bonbons on the candy table were arranged in round boxes covered with crepe paper roses. Those operating the booths wore similarly themed clothing, with the young ladies at the flower booth dressed in gowns the same color as the flowers and the young men at the candy booth wearing square caps and white aprons.

Food included strawberries in every style and form: strawberry ice cream, strawberries and cream, strawberry-topped ice cream, strawberry whip (a light, airy dessert combining strawberries, confectioners' sugar, and egg whites), strawberry tarts and cakes, strawberry lemonade, strawberry sherbet, and, of course, strawberry shortcake.

Strawberries and Cream

This decadent treat was a popular Gilded Age dessert, featured not only at strawberry fetes and festivals, but also at tea parties and kettledrums—informal afternoon or early evening social parties featuring a light meal. When served at a kettledrum, it was often accompanied by sponge cake *(see page 169)**. This recipe is adapted from* Household Words, *a weekly literary magazine edited by Charles Dickens from 1850 to 1859 and revived by his son Charles Dickens Jr. in the 1880s, continuing until 1905.*

SERVES 4–6

1 (16-ounce) package fresh strawberries, washed and hulled

⅓ cup sugar

1½ cups heavy cream, divided

Place strawberries in a large, deep bowl. Gently crush the berries using the back of a fork or a pastry cutter until they are a chunky, soupy consistency. Sprinkle the sugar on top, then pour ½ cup cream over the sugar-sweetened berries. Stir until thoroughly combined. Place in the refrigerator to keep cool.

Pour the remaining 1 cup heavy cream into a large bowl and whip using an electric mixer on medium speed until soft peaks form, about 4–5 minutes.

Remove strawberries from the refrigerator and transfer to a glass bowl or individual dishes. Spoon cream over the strawberries, using the back of the spoon to create a swirly pattern if desired.

Strawberry Shortcake

True strawberry shortcake incorporates a rich, crumbly, biscuit-like cake that is not too sweet—very similar to a scone. The biscuit dough can be shaped into one large cake and then cut into pieces, or baked as separate little cakes, either by cutting the dough into rounds with a biscuit cutter or dropping spoonfuls of dough on a baking sheet like a drop biscuit. Each individual cake is then split in half, filled with ripe, juicy strawberries, and topped with fresh whipped cream. If you can, try to find local strawberries for this recipe, as they will be fresher, juicier, and more flavorful. This recipe is easy and requires minimal ingredients. The biscuits are delicious and can be served on their own—as part of a chicken dinner, paired with other summer fruit such as blueberries or peaches, or even for breakfast.

SERVES 6

FOR THE SHORTCAKE:

1 (16-ounce) package fresh strawberries

2 tablespoons sugar, divided

2 cups all-purpose flour

¼ teaspoon salt

3 tablespoons chilled butter, cut into ½-inch pieces

1 teaspoon baking soda

¾ cup sour cream

1 egg, beaten

FOR THE WHIPPED CREAM:

1 cup heavy cream

2 tablespoons confectioners' sugar

½ teaspoon vanilla

Preheat oven to 375°F. Place a mixing bowl and beaters in the freezer (for making whipped cream later).

Rinse, hull, and slice the strawberries. Place in a medium bowl and sprinkle with 1 tablespoon sugar. Stir gently just to coat the berries. Set aside.

Mix the remaining 1 tablespoon sugar, flour, and salt together, then add the chilled butter, blending it in with a pastry cutter or two knives until the mixture is a fine consistency.

Strawberry Shortcake

Combine the baking soda and sour cream in a small bowl and add to the other ingredients. Add the beaten egg and mix with a fork until a soft dough forms, adding more flour a tablespoon at a time if the dough seems sticky.

Form the dough into a ball with floured hands and roll out onto a lightly floured surface to ¾-inch thickness. Cut into 4 biscuits with a biscuit cutter and place on a baking sheet lined with parchment paper. Scoop up the remaining dough and roll it out again, cutting out 2 more biscuits. Add to the baking sheet and place in the oven.

Bake for 15 minutes, then remove the biscuits from the oven and place on a wire rack to cool.

To make the whipped cream, remove the mixing bowl and beaters from the freezer. Add the heavy cream, confectioners' sugar, and vanilla to the bowl and whip using an electric mixer on medium speed for about 5 minutes or until firm peaks form.

To serve, split the 6 shortcakes in half with a serrated knife and place each bottom half on a dessert plate. Spoon about ⅓ cup of the strawberries and their juice on each bottom portion, and top with a large spoonful of whipped cream and then the shortcake tops. Garnish with additional strawberries and whipped cream if desired.

ICE CREAM SOCIALS

Ice cream socials were another beloved outdoor activity during the Gilded Age, typically held on the grounds of schools and churches as fund-raisers, similar to strawberry festivals. In the absence of air-conditioning, ice cream was one way to keep cool in the summer. Men would wear wide-brimmed hats and women long white dresses, seeking shade under trees, while children would line up in eager anticipation of the day's main attraction: ice cream.

Ice cream and other types of socials were meant to entertain large numbers of people. In addition to serving as fund-raisers, they were also held as community events, giving folks the opportunity to catch up with their neighbors, and as theme parties, based on a theme such as music or games. A band or other form of musical entertainment often played before or during the refreshments. Late nineteenth-century newspapers are chock-full of announcements about upcoming ice cream socials and write-ups of those that had already occurred.

All of this was made possible because of nineteenth-century technological advances. Sugar became more affordable and available in the mid-1800s due to improvements in sugar processing and the development of beet sugar. Then in 1843, American Nancy Johnson invented an ice cream freezer for home use. It featured a crank and a dasher inside the stirring pot so that the ice cream could be churned without having to open the pot. Johnson's invention made ice cream making easier and more obtainable to the masses (in the past it was

---

Ladies Aid Societies

Gilded Age ice cream socials were often hosted by Ladies Aid Societies. Born out of the desire of women to help with the Civil War effort, these aid associations were formed by ladies in both the North and the South. They would collect donations such as food, clothing, and medical supplies and performed duties such as rolling bandages, making cartridges, and preparing sandbags. Some women began to help as nurses. After the war, many societies continued to provide assistance to war veterans and their families. Eventually they expanded their charitable service activities through affiliations with churches and synagogues, which included hosting ice cream socials and other events to raise money for various causes.

The Ice Cream Cone

Throughout most of the Gilded Age, the frozen treats at ice cream socials would have been handed out in glass dishes or paper cones, which were available by the 1850s. But by the turn of the twentieth century, a new way to serve ice cream came on the scene that was portable, convenient, and edible: the ice cream cone. Although the first patent for a mold to make wafer-type cones was issued in 1903 in New York to water ice vendor Italo Marchiony, it wasn't until the 1904 World's Fair in St. Louis that the concept of the ice cream cone as a new way to eat ice cream began to circulate widely throughout the United States. According to lore, Syrian immigrant Ernest Hamwi was selling *zalabia* (Persian waffles) next to an ice cream stand and he (or his friend Abe Doumar) had the idea to combine the two confections by rolling the waffles into a cone and filling them with ice cream. After the fair, Hamwi began working with the Cornucopia Waffle Company and similar companies to market this novelty.

Cornucopia Waffle Oven Company trademark, 1905 COURTESY OF MISSOURI STATE ARCHIVES

much more labor-intensive and time-consuming). She later sold the rights to her invention to kitchen wholesaler William Young for $200 because she lacked the finances to produce it. He marketed the machine as the "Johnson Patent Ice-Cream Freezer."

As demand for ice cream increased, bigger and more complex machinery was introduced to manufacture the frozen treat on a larger scale. By the 1880s, the launch of cooling systems based on absorption and condensation were game changers for ice cream production. In the 1890s, electric freezers and other equipment were introduced, although many did not take off until the early part of the twentieth century.

Although some flavors of ice cream that were favorites during the Gilded Age are still commonly served today, such as vanilla, lemon, strawberry, and coffee, others were quite different, based on the ingredients that were fashionable and available at the time. These included pineapple, sarsaparilla, ginger, nectar, raspberry, and biscuit glacé (made using sponge cake as a thickener). The ice cream would have been made by combining fresh or preserved fruits or syrups with white sugar, cream or milk, and eggs (if the custard variety). The ubiquitous chocolate didn't enter the mainstream until the end of the nineteenth century when improvements in cacao bean processing allowed for a better-tasting and more affordable product.

Strawberry Ice Cream

This luscious ice cream is based on a recipe from Philadelphia confectioner and restaurateur James Parkinson, who had a reputation for producing the city's finest ice creams from the 1840s through the 1890s. Philadelphia-style ice cream was traditionally made with just fresh cream, sugar, and fruit or some other flavoring. Parkinson stressed that the cream should be "absolutely fresh, pure, rich and sweet," and "only the best white sugar and finest and purest flavors to be obtained" should be used. In his opinion, Philadelphia ice cream "smacked of the fat of the land."

1 (16-ounce) package fresh strawberries, washed and hulled

4 cups heavy cream

1½ cups sugar

½ cup freshly squeezed orange juice (from 2 medium oranges)

Place the strawberries in a large, deep bowl and mash gently using the back of a fork or a pastry blender so they are a chunky consistency. Add the cream, sugar, and orange juice and mix until well combined.

Pour mixture into the chilled bowl of an ice cream maker and mix until frozen as per ice cream maker manufacturer's instructions. Transfer to a glass bowl and store in the freezer until ready to serve.

Wafers à la Française

Paper-thin, light, and delicately curled, wafers date back to the Middle Ages, when they were served at banquet meals and hawked on street corners throughout Europe. These early versions were likely thicker than today's wafers—more like waffles. Over time, wafer batter became thinner, producing an airy, lightweight cookie that was rolled into a cylindrical shape by curling around a wooden rod or rolling pin while still warm. In the nineteenth century it became popular to serve these feather-like delicacies alongside cool, creamy ice cream and rich puddings. *(See photo on next page.)*

MAKES 3½ DOZEN

- 1 stick (½ cup) unsalted butter
- ½ cup milk
- 2 egg whites
- ½ cup sugar
- 1 cup all-purpose flour
- 1 tablespoon orange flower water (or rosewater, vanilla, or almond extract)

Heat oven to 350°F. Have ready some rolling pins, bottles, or thin glasses (champagne flutes work well).

Melt the butter and combine with the milk. In a separate bowl, whisk the egg whites until frothy, about 1–2 minutes, then stir in the sugar and flour until well mixed. Add the butter and milk mixture a little at a time, and then add the orange flower water. The batter should be thin, like a crepe—if it seems too thick, add a little more milk to thin it out.

Drop tablespoons of the batter one at a time onto parchment paper–lined baking sheets. Spread each portion with a spoon or tip of a knife to a diameter of about 3 inches.

Bake for 12–15 minutes until cookies begin to brown around the edges, rotating once during baking. Remove the baking sheets and while still warm, carefully remove wafers from the sheet with a large spatula and drape over the rolling pins, bottles, or glasses so that they curve around the cylinder, creating a rolled shape.

When cool, transfer the rolled wafers to a wire rack to harden completely. Serve with ice cream.

French Vanilla Ice Cream

This custardy classic is adapted from New York Cooking School founder and instructor Juliet Corson's recipe for "French Ice-Cream." French ice creams often involved heating cream and milk with egg yolks to make a rich custard, whereas "English" ice creams were uncooked and did not include eggs. Corson often recommended "over-sweetening" her ice cream recipes, perhaps to ensure the sweetness was not dulled too much during the freezing process. Feel free to adjust the sugar amount based on your preference.

SERVES 8

2 cups heavy cream
2 cups 2% milk
1 vanilla bean
6 egg yolks
1¼ cups sugar

Pour cream and milk into a large heavy pot. Split vanilla bean lengthwise and scrape out seeds. Add seeds and bean to the pot. Place over medium heat and cook until a skin forms across the surface and it reaches 170°F on a candy thermometer, about 5–7 minutes. Remove from the burner and allow to cool.

While cream and milk are cooling, place egg yolks and sugar in a large mixing bowl and stir with a wire whisk until smooth, about 1 minute. The mixture will be thick, like a paste.

When the cream mixture has cooled to 110°F (after about 15–20 minutes), slowly add the egg yolks and sugar to the pot. Heat on medium until it begins to thicken and small bubbles form around the edges, stirring frequently, about 3–5 minutes. Do not bring to a boil.

Remove the mixture from the heat and strain through a fine sieve into a mixing bowl. Place the mixing bowl on top of a larger bowl filled with ice, stirring frequently to cool it down, about 10–15 minutes.

Pour the mixture into the chilled bowl of an ice cream maker and mix until frozen as per ice cream maker manufacturer's instructions. Transfer to a glass bowl and store in the freezer until ready to serve.

CHAPTER THREE

DINING OUT

SOCIAL CLUBS

Fish House Punch
Crown Roast of Lamb with Mint Sauce
Bermuda Potatoes with Parsley Sauce
Marble Cake

RISE OF THE RESTAURANT

Waldorf Salad
Rabbit, Hunter Style
Meringues à la Crème
Apple Fritters with Wine Sauce

BANQUET DINNERS

Oysters on the Half Shell
Pot-au-Feu
Chicken Salad
Chocolate Jelly

BALLS

Lobster Fricassee
Charlotte Russe
Chilled Green Bean Salad

The first dinner of the Clover Club of Philadelphia—January 19, 1882—may be looked upon as the beginning of the era of the American roast.

—RAY BROADUS BROWNE, *RITUALS AND CEREMONIES IN POPULAR CULTURE*, 1980

THE GILDED AGE was a time in America's history that glittered with magnificent wealth on the surface, but bubbled underneath with corruption and social issues. Finance, culture, and cuisine were dominant themes. Stylish and sophisticated restaurants that catered to the wealthy began to pop up in major cities. Exclusive eating clubs were popular places to socialize and negotiate business deals, and banquet dinners and balls were de rigueur ways to flaunt prosperity and status. This chapter features recipes from these popular Gilded Age establishments.

SOCIAL CLUBS

In America's early days, taverns provided places to eat and drink, but the selections were often limited. Most served as central meeting places where men could conduct business. During the early eighteenth century, Philadelphia's elite upper-class merchants and influential leaders took this idea one step further, creating a number of exclusive establishments where they could meet, share information, and socialize while enjoying a good meal, a concept borrowed from London's famed "gentlemen's clubs." By the time of the Gilded Age, these clubs were thriving hubs of activity. Many still continue to this day.

One of the best known is the Philadelphia Club, considered the oldest metropolitan gentlemen's club in the United States. Founded in 1834, members have met at the Thomas Butler Mansion at 1301 Walnut Street since 1850. During the Gilded Age, one of the club's lunch menu staples was oyster fritters served alongside chicken salad, a combination that soon extended to other private gentlemen's clubs throughout the city. Each of these clubs had a slightly different focus, with topics and interests ranging from political issues and charitable intentions to art, literature, music, science, and even horseback riding. But the most significant and plentiful were the eating clubs, also called dining or "glutton" clubs.

BY THE NUMBERS

Many New York social clubs had strict rules regarding membership and would cap participants at a certain number. Some membership rolls were larger, such as New York's University Club with two thousand members and the Union League and the Union Club, each with one thousand. But they were still very exclusive, with one observer noting in 1887 that "membership in the Union implies social recognition and the highest respectability." Other clubs were even more restrictive. The Democratic Party–focused Manhattan Club limited its membership to six hundred, and the Society of Patriarchs, founded by society maven Ward McAllister in 1872, started with a roster of just twenty-five men, although it was expanded to fifty in the 1880s, including the addition of Cornelius Vanderbilt II and J. P. Morgan. But perhaps the most exclusive of all was Newport's Gooseberry Island Fishing Club, with membership restricted to just fourteen of America's wealthiest men, with surnames such as Vanderbilt, Belmont, Fish, and Dyer.

The Clover Club and Mark Twain

Philadelphia's Clover Club was formed in 1882 as an "association of prominent men who like a good dinner, and who also like to see their friends enjoy one." They chose the upscale Hotel Bellevue on Broad Street as their headquarters. Meals were served on a four-leaf-clover-shaped table, reserved exclusively for the club's monthly dinners. The atmosphere was fun and jovial. Guests were often invited to partake in the merriment and delicious food, such as the dinner Mark Twain attended in 1885, which featured dishes such as littleneck clams; printantère à la royale (a consommé of early summer vegetables cut in dainty shapes, with green peas and asparagus tips); hors d'oeuvres varies (a selection of appetizers); truites de ruisseau à la maître d'hotel (brook trout); pommes de terre à la brabant (fried potatoes with parsley); bouchees à la béchamel (petite pastry puffs filled with cheese béchamel); selle d'agneau de printemps, sauce menthe (saddle of spring lamb with mint sauce); betteraves nouvelles au beurre (buttered beets); petits pois nouveaux (petite peas); sorbet au benefice des acteurs (sorbet "for the benefit of the actors"); and becassines roties sur canapés au cresson (canapés of snipe on toast with watercress). Twain was a little surprised by the outspoken, raucous behavior of the Clover Club members, which he claimed went on for five hours.

Menu

COTUIT OYSTERS

PUREE FERMIERE

HORS-D'OEUVRES

SILVER PERCH BELLEVUE
BERMUDA POTATOES

LOVING CUP

SADDLE OF DARBY MUTTON
MASHED TURNIPS
LIMA BEANS

BELL PUNCH

RAIL BIRDS
FROZEN TOMATOES MAYONNAISE

CLOVER ICES

FANCY CAKES

COFFEE

MOET & CHANDON
WHITE SEAL
CHAMPAGNE
SPECIAL VINTAGE
1900

The Bellevue-Stratford
Thursday, October 17, 1907

Clover Club Dinner Menu, 1907 NEW YORK PUBLIC LIBRARY

The Black Elite

A small but significant elite class of African Americans had their own social circle of activity in New York City during the Gilded Age. Many had moved to Brooklyn following the Civil War and found work as carpenters, shoemakers, tailors, teachers, ministers, doctors, and pharmacists. They founded newspapers, literary societies, political associations, and schools. Just like the white upper class, they hosted elaborate social occasions, such as debutante parties, banquet dinners, and balls, and took summer excursions to Newport or Long Island. And they enjoyed a thriving social club scene, with annual dinners such as the one held by the tongue-in-cheek New York and Newport Ugly Fishing Club. The club's dinner in 1883 was a multi-course meal featuring oysters paired with sauterne wine, mock turtle soup, salmon with hollandaise sauce, roast turkey paired with Champagne, ham with Champagne sauce, a palate-cleansing course of Roman punch, canvasback duck with currant jelly, grouse paired with sherry, celery with mayonnaise, cheese and crackers, tutti-frutti ice cream, Italian cream, and a final course of coffee, cognac, and cigars. The evening included discussions on a variety of topics ranging from politics and business to Africa, humor, education, and poetry, as well as several speeches, singing, and a parting poem.

One of these, the now-defunct Pee Wee Club, was popular in the 1870s. The group met on Saturday evenings promptly at 6:30 p.m., receiving sherry and bitters upon arrival to whet the palate for the extensive dinner to come. One menu from 1875 featured delicacies such as clams, soup à la printanière (a light soup of asparagus tips and spring vegetables, cut into fancy shapes), Delaware shad with crab sauce and cucumbers, potatoes Parisienne, saddle of lamb with mint sauce, roast capons, fresh peas, Bermuda potatoes, relishes and tomatoes, asparagus, English snipes, lettuce and cheese, and ice cream and coffee. Cordials, brandy, and sherry bitters were served, along with Barsac, Scharzhofberger, Château Margaux, sherry, Madeira, and Champagne wines. The price tag for the food, wine, table decorations, and wait service for sixteen "gents" totaled $173.40, approximately $4,600 in today's dollars.

All-male dining clubs of varying types cropped up in other US locations as well, particularly areas where wealth and exclusivity thrived. These clubs were typically secretive and private, with an air of aristocracy and a restrictive membership dictated by club rules designed to keep "undesirables" out. One example was the Hoboken Turtle Club, founded in 1796 by Colonel John Stevens, the American lawyer, engineer, and inventor who was instrumental in launching steam-powered trains and boats in the United States. The club met twice a year near Hoboken's Elysian Fields in northern New Jersey to dine on turtle, one of the most popular and fashionable foods from the 1600s through the early 1900s. Turtle Club members were expected to help prepare the meal, which typically included turtle soup and turtle steaks, often made from those caught in the nearby Hudson River. By the 1870s, the group began meeting in various New York locations, managing to keep the club together until the 1940s, when they disbanded.

New York's thriving social scene in the nineteenth century opened the door for all kinds of eating clubs, such as the Blot Club, named after the venture's creator, Chef Pierre Blot of the New York Cooking Academy. While the club had a social bent, its true focus was on the food, with particular emphasis on healthfulness, taste, convenience, neatness, and cost. Members paid $5 for a club subscription, and then nominal amounts for each meal. Dinner times were staggered in order to accommodate all members, with initial subscribers securing the first choice of time slots. Its dining rooms were immaculately clean and tastefully carpeted and furnished, and the kitchen was "entirely open to view" as a way to enforce the idea of pristine spotlessness. Although the club had a positive start, attaining a roster of over one thousand members within a month, it never got a chance to take off. Apparently, a dispute between Blot and the club caused the enterprise to end abruptly. Perhaps New York was just not ready for this type of practical minded, reasonably priced eating club alongside all the Gilded Age excessiveness.

Fish House Punch

Philadelphia's Fish House Club, also known as the Colony in Schuylkill or Schuylkill Fishing Company, was founded in 1732 as a men's fishing club by a few of the city's original settlers. The small group's intent was to "spend an idyllic day every now and then dawdling on the banks of the Schuylkill River . . . shooting game birds and fishing and cooking their catch for dinner, with no wives or servants present." Although city development, pollution, and overfishing have caused the club to move its location several times over the years, the citizens (as club members are called) still gather along the Schuylkill to feast on barbecued pork, grilled steaks, planked shad, and perch "thrown" in skillets, all prepared by club members and served with the group's famous (and very potent) Fish House Punch.

Crushed ice
1 tablespoon lemon juice
1 tablespoon sugar
1½ ounces brandy
1 ounce light rum
1 ounce peach brandy
Lemon slice for garnish

Fill a cocktail shaker halfway with crushed ice. Add the lemon juice, sugar, brandy, rum, and peach brandy. Shake well to mix ingredients, then strain into a stemless wine or cocktail glass. Garnish with a slice of lemon.

Crown Roast of Lamb with Mint Sauce

Lamb was a popular dish during the Gilded Age, especially when it was in season. But the cuts of meat generally served at the time were large forequarters, roasts, or legs of lamb, which are harder to find in today's markets. A diagram in The White House Cookbook *(1887) includes a page-long instruction for carving a forequarter of lamb into nine pieces, ending with "the carver should always ascertain whether the guest prefers ribs, brisket, or a piece of the shoulder." The idea was that a large piece of meat would have been a showpiece for the table and signify one's status. This crown roast recipe, adapted by food historian and culinary stylist Dan Macey, is an eye-appealing showstopper that will have guests cheering when brought to the table.*

SERVES 8–10

¼ cup chopped fresh rosemary

2 teaspoons chopped fresh thyme

2 tablespoons chopped fresh oregano

6 garlic cloves, minced

1 tablespoon salt

2 teaspoons pepper

1 (4–5 pound) crown roast of lamb, or 2 (2-pound) racks (see note below)

Olive oil

Preheat oven to 425°F.

Combine rosemary, thyme, oregano, garlic, salt, and pepper in a small bowl.

Place crown roast on a wire cooling rack placed on top of a baking sheet. Rub olive oil all over the roast, both inside and outside, then rub the herb mixture all over the lamb. Cover the bones loosely with a sheet of aluminum foil.

Crown Roast of Lamb with Mint Sauce

CONTINUED

Place roast in the oven on the lower rack and cook until a thermometer inserted into the thickest part of the lamb registers 125–130°F, about 20–30 minutes. Transfer the lamb to a serving platter and let stand for 5–10 minutes before bringing it to the table to carve. Serve with mint sauce. (You could also serve the lamb with prepared mint jelly and let your guests spoon the jelly over the chops while warm, which allows the jelly to melt.)

MRS. RORER'S MINT SAUCE

This recipe is adapted from Philadelphia Cooking School instructor Sarah Tyson Rorer. Mrs. Rorer recommended serving lamb with mint sauce, green peas, and asparagus tips.

1 bunch (about 10 stalks) fresh mint

1 tablespoon sugar

½ teaspoon salt

Pinch of black pepper

4 teaspoons vinegar

Chop mint until very fine. Place in a small bowl and mix with sugar, salt, and pepper, then stir in vinegar.

NOTE: *It is easiest to preorder the crown roast of lamb, which is two racks of lamb tied together with twine and trimmed so it will form into a circle. Generally, a butcher or even the meat departments of supermarkets will have a crown roast of lamb available, especially during winter holidays. You can make the crown yourself by trussing two 7–9 rib racks together and cutting one-third of the way through the flesh of each bone.*

Bermuda Potatoes with Parsley Sauce

Bermuda potatoes were highly prized in the Gilded Age, as they were often the first variety of new potatoes to arrive in American markets each spring, typically in March or April. Petite in size with thin skins, they were considered delicate and flavorful. Thomas De Voe describes them as red-skinned potatoes in his book The Market Assistant *(1867), but any color or type of small new potato would work fine in this recipe.*

SERVES 4–6

1 (1½-pound) package new potatoes
1 tablespoon unsalted butter
1 tablespoon all-purpose flour
1 cup milk
1 teaspoon salt
½ teaspoon pepper
1 tablespoon finely chopped fresh parsley

Place potatoes in a colander and rinse under cold water, scrubbing off any dirt with a soft brush.

Transfer potatoes to a medium pot and add enough water to cover. Bring water to a boil over high heat. Once boiling, turn heat down to medium-low and simmer for 10–15 minutes until fork tender. Drain potatoes in a colander. Rinse the pot and wipe dry.

Prepare the sauce by melting butter in the pot over medium heat. Add flour, whisking until smooth, then pour in milk. Continue to whisk until mixture comes to a boil and thickens in consistency, about 5 minutes. Remove from heat and add salt, pepper, and parsley. Stir to combine.

Transfer potatoes to a bowl or low dish. Pour parsley sauce over potatoes. Serve immediately.

Marble Cake

Marble cake typically conjures up images of a beautifully swirled vanilla and chocolate cake, similar to the look of vanilla fudge ice cream. However, throughout most of the nineteenth century, the swirls in marble cake got their lovely chestnut color from molasses and rich spices such as nutmeg, cinnamon, and cloves, not chocolate. By the early twentieth century, chocolate eclipsed many other ingredients, evolving into the extremely popular flavor that it is today. This cake has several steps and ingredients, but its delicious taste is well worth the extra effort.

- 4 large eggs, separated
- 2 sticks (1 cup) unsalted butter, softened
- 1 cup granulated sugar
- ½ cup milk
- 4 cups cake flour
- 1½ teaspoons baking powder
- 1 cup brown sugar
- ½ cup molasses
- ¼ cup sour cream
- ½ teaspoon baking soda
- 1 teaspoon ground nutmeg
- 1 teaspoon cinnamon
- ½ teaspoon allspice
- ¼ teaspoon cloves

Preheat oven to 350°F. Butter a Bundt pan or two 8 x 4-inch loaf pans and dust with flour.

For the light part: Using a hand or stand mixer, beat egg whites in a large glass or stainless steel bowl until foamy, about 2–3 minutes. Set aside.

Place one of the sticks of butter in a large bowl and beat on medium-high speed until light, about 1 minute. Add granulated sugar ¼ cup at a time, beating 20–30 seconds after each addition. Turn the mixer to low and slowly add the milk and egg whites, beating until well mixed.

Sift 2 cups of the cake flour with the baking powder in a small bowl. Slowly add a little at a time to the wet ingredients until thoroughly incorporated. Set aside.

CONTINUED

For the dark part: In a separate bowl, beat the remaining stick of butter with the brown sugar and molasses on medium-high speed until creamy. Turn down to medium and add the sour cream and egg yolks until well mixed.

Sift the remaining 2 cups cake flour with the baking soda, nutmeg, cinnamon, allspice, and cloves. With the mixer running on low speed, add the flour mixture in ¼ cup increments to the wet mixture.

To make the cake: Pour the light and dark batter in the pan(s) in alternate intervals. When done, run a knife through the batter a few times to create a swirly pattern.

Bake for 50–60 minutes or until a toothpick inserted into the top comes out clean. Place pan(s) on a wire rack to cool, about 30 minutes for a Bundt pan and 15 minutes for loaf pans, then invert on the wire rack to cool completely. Ice with a sugary glaze if desired.

GLAZE

1 cup confectioners' sugar

3 tablespoons milk or cream

1 teaspoon vanilla

Mix sugar, milk, and vanilla in a small bowl and drizzle over top of cake.

RISE OF THE RESTAURANT

Rod's Steak and Seafood Grille, The Madison Hotel, Morristown, New Jersey

Great numbers of immigrants entered the United States in the mid-nineteenth century, bringing with them the foods and cultures of myriad nations, including France, Ireland, Italy, Germany, and China. This was especially true in New York, which was the first point of entry for many. An expanding metropolis in the midst of a major population boom, Manhattan's population reached one million by 1860, tripling in size from twenty years earlier. To keep up with the steady stream of people flowing into the city, New York's restaurant and hotel industries multiplied at a rapid pace. An 1847 city tourist guide estimated the total number of New York restaurants at a little over one hundred (not counting the numerous Oyster Houses and Cellars scattered throughout the city), but by the 1860s there were over five thousand. These included both sophisticated establishments that catered to the wealthy and basic eateries for the growing middle class.

As New York entered the Gilded Age era, it began to dominate other American cities in terms of finance, culture, and cuisine. Sporting a flourishing entertainment district with hotels, restaurants, and theaters, Manhattan was blossoming into a stylish city, with its broad Parisian-style boulevards and upscale shops lining Ladies' Mile on Sixth Avenue. Linked to

Sherry's

Louis Sherry was a smart and savvy entrepreneur with his finger on the pulse of the desires and expectations of the Gilded Age elite. Intuitive and attentive, he absorbed every detail of the restaurant industry, eventually becoming one of the most revered and connected restaurateurs of the era. He learned all about French cuisine working as a busboy and waiter at New York's Brunswick Hotel on Fifth Avenue and 26th Street, and then landed a summer job managing the Hotel Elberon beach resort in Long Branch, New Jersey, in 1880. This led to the opening of a New York confectionery store and catering business that supplied elaborate parties for the Gilded Age's famous "Four Hundred" (see page 135), intimate dinners for J. P. Morgan, and meals for the Narragansett Pier Casino in Rhode Island. By 1890 he had opened Sherry's, a Fifth Avenue restaurant located directly across from Delmonico's, his main competitor. It featured a large public dining room, a ballroom, and several private dining rooms that played host to balls and suppers for wealthy society families. The Astors were among Sherry's regular customers, with Caroline Astor the first to give a ball there, and whose endorsement sealed Sherry's place among New York's upper class. In fact, it was rumored that Sherry was backed by the Astors' funding, although he maintained he climbed the ladder to success by "giving people the novelties that my competitors neglected."

Sherry's Restaurant, 1906. WIKIMEDIA COMMONS

an ever-expanding network of trains and fast steamships, the availability of many foods such as beef, fish, eggs, and out-of-season fruits and vegetables significantly increased. Restaurants benefited from both the large variety of foods available in the city's markets and America's post–Civil War industrial innovations and booming enterprises.

In addition, New Yorkers were becoming increasingly food-focused and fascinated with everything epicurean, particularly French cuisine. French words like *restaurant*, *menu*, *café*, and *à la* dishes were becoming increasingly familiar, as shown by the popularity of Delmonico's, launched in the mid-1820s as a wine shop/confectionery by two Swiss brothers, John (Giovanni) and Peter (Pietro) Del-Monico. The concept was so successful, they were able to open up a Parisian-style restaurant next door in 1831, hiring a French chef and bringing in their young nephew Lorenzo to serve as a manager. This kicked off a Delmonico family restaurant dynasty with locations scattered throughout the city.

The Delmonico's on Fifth Avenue and 14th Street was particularly well known for hosting high society events and dinners for influential gentlemen. For example, when Charles Dickens came to the United States for his second speaking tour in 1867, he was famously feted there by the American press. About two hundred men were in attendance—all the leading authors, editors, and publishers at the time, including Horace Greeley of the *New York Tribune* (who presided over the festivities), Henry James Raymond (co-founder of the *New York Times*), Charles Scribner, Thomas Nast, J. B. Lippincott, and Henry Holt. The room where the dinner was held was decorated in both British and

If in an average company you select at random a dozen men and a dozen women, the masculine group will possess much more knowledge of cookery. . . . Go into a restaurant, with a number of men and women. Unless there should chance to be in the company a woman who has traveled extensively and observed much, you will never go wrong if you entrust the selection of the dinner to the gentleman.

—JULIET CORSON, COOKING INSTRUCTOR

Cooks creating pièces montées *and* pâté d'office *(confectioners' paste) in the confectionery section of the Delmonico's kitchen, 1902* WIKIMEDIA COMMONS

American colors, including vases of fresh flowers and *pièces montées* (elaborate confectionary sculptures) representing the two nations. The cover of the bill of fare featured small medallions imprinted with cupids holding up a circle with the banquet's date: April 18, 1868. The menu inside was written in French and printed in rich plum-hued ink. Created by Delmonico's Chef Charles Ranhofer, it was extensive and uniquely themed to the occasion, with Les Petites Tim-balles à la Dickens (small pastry molds) as hors d'oeuvres, entrées such as Cotelettes à la Fenimore Cooper (lamb chops), a palate-cleansing Sorbet a l'Americaine, and Gâteaux Savarins et Viennois (Savarin and Viennese cakes).

Ordering Boeuf, Poulet et Poisson

Reading a menu, whether it be at a fancy restaurant, banquet, or dinner party during the Gilded Age, required the diner to be able to read French. American high society embraced all things French, especially when it came to food and entertaining. When restaurants began to proliferate across America in the second half of the nineteenth century, New York's Delmonico's set the standard by presenting the menu in French. Other restaurants soon followed in the same vein. Even more humble establishments outside of large cities would at least list their courses in French.

MENU

Chaud

Consommé
Bouchées à la régence
Croquettes de chapons
Huitres, béchamel aux truffes
Terrapène à la Maryland
Canards à tête rouge
Thé & Café

Froid

Saumon à la parisienne
Filets de boeuf à la Lucullus
Galantines de poulet à la Victoria
Langues de boeuf à l'écarlate
Aspic de foies-gras, historié
Pâté de bécasses, Pithivier
Cailles piquées, grouse
Mayonnaise de volaille
Salade de homard
Sandwiches
Rillettes
Canapés

Entremets de douceur

Gelée aux cerises — Oublies à la crême
Gateau noisette — Pain d'abricots
Mottoes — Pièces montées — Bonbons
Glaces de fantaisies
Tutti-frutti — Biscuit glacé
Dessert — Petits fours — Fruits

Vins

Moët Impérial Brut — Pommery sec
Pontet Canet — Apollinaris

Le 20 Décembre, 1888
DELMONICOS

Dinner held at Delmonico's, 1888 NEW YORK PUBLIC LIBRARY

The French cooking style was all the rage. Heavy cream and butter sauces accompanied many dishes, and pastries and fancy gâteaux were popular desserts. Since most of the haute cuisine dishes of the time were French named, it also made sense to print the entire menu in French as well as course categories. The French word *menu* actually replaced "bill of fare," which was used mostly prior to the Gilded Age. Ironically, the menus were often full of grammatical, spelling, or accent errors, as the Americans writing the menus were not actually all that fluent in French.

Properly referring to food by its French name was also an indication of one's status simply by being able to understand the menu and pronounce the French words. And the fact that only the well-educated and well-bred would have been proficient in the language made it even more popular with the upper class. Additionally, the food, when labeled in French, seemed much more appetizing. In 1904, Charles Fellow wanted to write his own culinary handbook and abstain from using French terms for both the food and the courses, claiming the use of English is "perfectly adequate in describing the dishes." But a menu item such as "frog legs in paper bags" just didn't have the same ring as *cuisses de grenouilles en papillote*.

These elegant new restaurants inspired even more elaborate dinner parties in wealthy homes, where hiring a French chef was considered *hauteur de la mode*—the height of fashion. Ward McCallister, the famed arbiter of social taste at the time, even offered advice to wealthy women when dealing with their notorious arrogant French chefs. "No French cook will take any interest in his work unless he receives praise and criticism; but above all things, you must know how to criticize," advises McCallister in his book, *Society as I Have Found It*. "If he finds you are able to appreciate his work when good, and condemn it when bad, he improves, and gives you something of value."

Contributed by food historian and culinary stylist Dan Macey

Waldorf Salad

Created by Oscar Tschirky in the late 1890s, the Waldorf Salad has had many iterations over the years. As maître d' of the Waldorf-Astoria, Tschirky was known for devising signature recipes for the restaurant, including this simple salad included in his 1896 cookbook, The Cook Book by "Oscar" of the Waldorf. *His original recipe featured just diced apples and celery "dressed with a good mayonnaise." Feel free to try the adapted homemade version below or use your favorite jarred mayonnaise. Chopped walnuts can be added for extra crunch.*

SERVES: 4

FOR THE SALAD:

2 large tart apples (like Granny Smith)

2 stalks celery

FOR THE MAYONNAISE DRESSING:

1 egg yolk (see note below)

½ teaspoon ground mustard

½ teaspoon salt

¼ teaspoon black pepper

2 teaspoons lemon juice

¾ cup olive or canola oil

OPTIONAL ITEMS FOR SERVING/GARNISH:

4 large apples

Boston or butterhead lettuce leaves, washed and dried

Peel apples and cut into ½-inch dice. Trim ends off celery and cut into ½-inch dice. Place apples and celery in a medium bowl and set aside.

To make the mayonnaise, place the egg yolk, mustard, salt, pepper, and lemon juice in a large deep bowl. Whisk very briskly until the mixture starts to form bubbles, about 1–2 minutes. Slowly add the olive oil a few drops at a time, stirring constantly with the whisk. When it starts to thicken and emulsify, add the oil in a steady stream, still whisking vigorously until all the oil has been added.

Combine about ½ cup of mayonnaise (or to taste) with the apples and celery. Stir to coat.

Waldorf Salad

Continued

For a fancy presentation, serve in apple cups. Using a paring knife, cut a circle around the stem end of 4 apples. Scoop out the center with a melon baller or small spoon so that each apple is a thin-walled cup. (The inside part of the apple can be strained through a sieve to remove any core or pits and used to make applesauce or pudding.) If desired, cut the top edge of the apple cups into a zigzag pattern. Place the apple cups in cold water until ready to serve.

To serve, drain apple cups and wipe dry. Spoon Waldorf Salad into cups and place on Boston or butterhead lettuce leaves.

NOTE: *To avoid the risk of salmonella, use pasteurized eggs.*

Rabbit, Hunter Style

This recipe was adapted by Chef Adam Diltz of Elwood restaurant in Philadelphia, who specializes in re-creating and revitalizing historic Pennsylvania cuisine. It was originally featured in The Epicurean, *the 1893 cookbook by Delmonico's Chef Charles Ranhofer. As per Chef Diltz, "while this dish may not be the most pretty by today's social media standards, the technique and flavor should definitely be brought back." Crimini mushrooms are also known as cremini mushrooms or baby bellas.*

SERVES 4–6

FOR THE RABBIT:

23 (about 1½ pounds) cremini mushrooms

2 tablespoons unsalted butter

1 quart (4 cups) veal or beef stock

2 tablespoons olive oil, divided

1 (2½–3 pound) rabbit, cut into 12 pieces

1 white onion, diced

8 ounces ham, diced

1 quart (4 cups) red wine

FOR THE ROUX:

1 stick (½ cup) unsalted butter

¾ cup all-purpose flour

FOR THE CROUTONS:

1 day-old French baguette

3 tablespoons unsalted butter

Clean the mushrooms by wiping gently with a damp paper towel or soft brush to remove surface dirt. Trim or discard any tough stems. Mince 15 of the mushrooms.

Melt 2 tablespoons butter in a large skillet over medium heat. Add the minced mushrooms and sauté for 5 minutes. Set aside.

Place veal stock in a deep saucepan and bring to a boil over medium-high heat. Use a teaspoon to gently remove the gills from the underside of the remaining mushrooms. Add the mushrooms to the stock and turn the heat down to low. Poach until the mushrooms are tender, about 3–5 minutes. Drain, reserving stock. Set aside.

Rabbit, Hunter Style

CONTINUED

Preheat oven to 325°F.

Heat 1 tablespoon olive oil in a large sautoir or heavy-bottomed sauté pan over medium-high heat. Add rabbit pieces and sear on all sides until browned (about 5 minutes per side). Remove pan from the heat and transfer rabbit to a plate. Cover with aluminum foil to keep warm.

Heat 1 tablespoon olive oil in the sautoir over low to medium heat. Add onions and ham and cook until the onions are soft and translucent, about 5–7 minutes. Add the rabbit pieces, reserved veal stock, and red wine. Cover with aluminum foil and place in the oven for about 1 hour or until the rabbit is tender. Strain and reserve the liquid, separating the rabbit from the onions and ham. Cover and keep warm.

Make a roux by melting 1 stick butter in a heavy-bottomed pot over medium-low heat. Add flour, stirring constantly with a wooden spoon for 6–7 minutes until it is brown in color.

Add the strained braising liquid to the roux and whisk vigorously. Bring to a boil, then turn the heat down to low and simmer for 10 minutes. Add the ham and onions to the liquid along with the cooked minced mushrooms.

To make the croutons, cut the bread into rectangular pieces about 1 by ¾ inch in size. Melt 3 tablespoons butter in a large sauté pan over medium-high heat. Add the bread cubes, stirring to coat with the butter. Spread them out in a single layer, toasting on one side for 1–2 minutes. Turn with a spatula so they brown on the other side. Continue cooking until brown and toasted on at least two sides. Remove from heat.

To plate, lay the rabbit pieces on a platter and pour the sauce over them. Garnish with the toasted croutons and poached mushrooms.

Meringues à la Crème

Meringues date back to the sixteenth century, when European cooks first realized that whisking egg whites with birch twigs (for the lack of a better utensil) created a light, frothy mixture. It was eventually discovered that meringue hardens when baked at a low temperature (or simply left out in the air to dry), changing the texture to one that is pleasantly airy and crispy. By the Gilded Age, meringues were available in a variety of shapes, sizes, and flavors, such as these bite-size treats lightly flavored with vanilla and filled with cream or jelly. This recipe was adapted from the 1893 cookbook Cooking for Profit *by chef and restaurateur Jessup Whitehead. Meant for those in the restaurant and hotel industries, it was originally published in the* San Francisco Daily Hotel Gazette.

MAKES ABOUT 6 DOZEN

6 egg whites, separated individually
Pinch of cream of tartar
2 cups granulated sugar
1 teaspoon vanilla extract

Preheat oven to 200°F.

Place 3 egg whites and cream of tartar in a large glass or stainless steel bowl. Beat on low speed with an electric mixer until soft peaks form, about 3–4 minutes, then increase speed to medium and add the sugar a little at a time.

Continue beating until the mixture looks like firm white cake icing (another 5–8 minutes). Add 2 more egg whites, one at a time, beating a few minutes between each until the meringue rises in stiff peaks when the beater is lifted from it. Add the vanilla and beat for about 30 seconds or until well mixed. Add the remaining egg white and beat another 30 seconds, just until incorporated.

Drop spoonfuls of meringue about an inch apart on baking sheets lined with parchment paper, being careful not to overcrowd.

Bake for 1½ hours with the oven door partly open if possible. The time will vary depending on the room temperature and humidity. They will be done when smooth and hard to the touch.

Remove from the oven and allow to cool on the baking sheets for 15 minutes, then transfer to wire racks to cool completely. When cool, scoop out the top part of each meringue and fill with whipped cream (see recipe on page 83) or your choice of fruit jelly.

Apple Fritters with Wine Sauce

These light and crispy pastries appeared on Gilded Age menus in a variety of ways. Typically dusted with confectioners' sugar and accompanied by a rum, brandy, or sherry sauce, our modern palates would assume they were served as a dessert, which was sometimes the case. But more often than not, they were served alongside meat and poultry dishes at upscale places such as the New York's Hotel Astor, the Quincy House in Boston, and the Ebbitt House in Washington, DC. As per the 1892 book The Art of Entertaining, *"apple fritters with sherry wine and sugar are very comforting things. The French name is* beignet de pomme.*"*

SERVES 8–10

2 cups all-purpose flour
4 teaspoons baking powder
½ teaspoon salt
2 tablespoons sugar
2 large eggs
6 tablespoons unsalted butter, melted
1½ cups milk
2 cups peeled and diced apples
2 cups vegetable oil

Sift flour, baking powder, salt, and sugar together in a large bowl. In a separate bowl, whisk eggs until foamy. Add butter and milk, mix well, and then add to dry ingredients. Stir to form a batter. Fold in apples.

Pour oil into a saucepan with high sides and place over medium-high heat. When it reaches 350°F on a candy thermometer, drop tablespoonfuls of the batter into the oil, about 6 to 8 at a time (do not overcrowd) and fry until golden brown on each side, about 2 minutes. Do not overcook, as the fritters will absorb too much oil and become soggy and greasy.

Remove fritters to a wire rack set over a baking sheet lined with paper towels or parchment paper to drain. Serve with wine sauce.

WINE SAUCE

1 stick (½ cup) unsalted butter, softened
1 cup confectioners' sugar
¼ cup sherry
Pinch of ground nutmeg

Place butter and sugar in a large mixing bowl and mix with an electric mixer on medium-high speed until creamy. Turn down to low and add sherry, beating until well mixed. Stir in nutmeg.

BANQUET DINNERS

Rooted in French and British aristocracy, the concept of fine dining was brought to America by its early colonists—the excellent food and wine enjoyed by Thomas Jefferson is one of the best-known examples. And due to the abundance of food that existed in the New World, it was not difficult to concoct meals of enormous proportions. Wealthy families commonly hosted lavish dinners in their own palatial homes, but it wasn't until the Gilded Age that dinners of great size and sophistication really began to flourish and take hold. The vast number of technological changes and developments during this time frame redefined class structures in America. More and more people had enough money to live in comfort and style, surrounded by a wide selection of purchased goods and services. The unique types of food they sought reflected these marked changes in dining habits as they navigated a complex and changing world.

Although they still entertained at home, the introduction of upscale restaurants like Delmonico's and Sherry's allowed wealthy tycoons and various organizations to host stylish banquets in a fine-dining establishment. Delmonico's was especially popular, quoted by the *New York Times* as being "the place where the great societies of New York have given their annual banquets, and where the great men who have visited New York have received compliment of a public dinner." This included banquets for the St. George, St. Nicholas, and St. Patrick New York societies, as well as annual alumni gatherings for Ivy League universities Yale, Harvard, Princeton, and Dartmouth. Delmonico's also hosted banquets for a plethora of Gilded Age luminaries, from Britain's Prince Arthur and the Grand Duke Alexis of Russia to inventor Samuel Morse and physicist John Tyndall.

But perhaps the most unique banquet meal ever served at Delmonico's was the "Swan Dinner" hosted by importer and ship-owner Edward Luckmeyer in 1873. This magnificent feast basically featured its own nature preserve. The seventy-two guests were seated around a huge oval table that contained a big lake in the center. An ornate gold cage made by Tiffany was positioned over the lake to house the main attraction—four stately white swans brought in from Brooklyn's Prospect Park. Miniature hills and valleys carpeted with delicate violets and other flowers encircled the lake. Tiny golden cages containing canary songbirds hung all around this enclosure and above the

Ballroom, Sherry's Restaurant, 1898 WIKIMEDIA COMMONS

table, filling the room with their melodies as the swans swam and splashed in the lake. Unfortunately the swans did not enjoy being penned in (it was also mating season) and staged a major battle during the meal.

This fanciful setting was so over the top that it almost overshadowed the impressive eight-course menu. Luckily Delmonico chef Charles Ranhofer recorded it in his 1,200-page masterpiece cookbook, *The Epicurean*. The eight courses began with two soups, consommé imperial (chicken-flavored consommé served with green peas, asparagus points, and small quenelles of chicken forcemeat) and velvety bisque aux crevettes (shrimp bisque). Next was a course of hors d'oeuvres, then fish (red snapper and roulades of smelt), a beef filet relevé, and an entrée course including canvasback duck and cold asparagus in a vinaigrette. At this point a pause was taken for a palate-cleansing sorbet, then the menu segued into the roast course of capon and saddle of mutton and a vegetable course of cardoons, choux fleurs sauce crème (cauliflower in cream sauce), and buttered peas. The meal ended with fifteen luscious dessert choices, from gelée de ananas (pineapple jelly) to gaufres chantilly (waffles with whipped cream), petits fours, and bonbons.

Sherry's was also host to numerous banquets, including an over-the-top dinner in 1903 where all of the guests dined while on horseback. Given by millionaire C. K. Billings in celebration of his election as president of the New York Equestrian Club, it was his intention to "give his clubmates the most memorable dinner that had yet been eaten." Billings originally wanted to serve his guests on horseback at his new stables in Washington Heights but claimed New York newspapers spoiled the surprise. So he pivoted to Sherry's, secretly arranging for the horses to be taken upstairs to the restaurant's second-floor ballroom by freight elevator two at a time. He hired drivers to pick up each guest and take them to Sherry's, where they enjoyed their first course in a banquet room on the ground floor. They were then led upstairs, where the horses were arranged in a horseshoe formation inside Sherry's grand ballroom, each equipped with a white quilted satin saddle and bridle and gold-and-white harness. In the center of the horseshoe was a woodland scene, with a mound of imitation green grass surrounded by flowers. Each saddle had a miniature table attached to the front to serve as a dining tray, as well as each guest's name printed in gold lettering to mark their place. The men mounted the horses, which stood patiently throughout the meal. Twelve courses in all were served by waiters dressed as hunting groomsmen, and while the men ate, so did the horses, munching on oats from individual satin-covered troughs. The tables were then removed so the guests could enjoy their after-dinner cigars and speeches. The *New York Times* called the dinner "one of the most novel that has ever been given in the city."

Dancing at the Waldorf-Astoria, *1896. Painting by Henry James Soulen.* WIKIMEDIA COMMONS

Eventually New York society had a whole "social season" that ran from November through February consisting of formal banquets and dinners located at certain hotels and restaurants, including the Waldorf-Astoria, the

Wining and Dining Competitions

Culinary contests were quite the rage among the Gilded Age upper class, particularly between Leonard Jerome (financier and maternal grandfather of Winston Churchill), William Travers (a wealthy Wall Street lawyer and investor), and banker August Belmont (founder of the Belmont Stakes horse race). The three men were in constant competition to see who could host the most extravagant gathering. Jerome offered fountains of Champagne and gold bejeweled bracelets tucked into every lady's napkin at a dinner held at his Madison Square house. Not to be outdone, Belmont handed out platinum bracelets to every lady guest at his next party. This competitive spirit carried over to locations outside their mansions, including one contest hosted by high society magnate Ward McAllister in 1867. Held at Delmonico's, this three-part contest was the result of bets exchanged among the three men, who were among the restaurant's best known patrons. Each gentleman staged their own dinner, attempting to top the other two. Known as the Gold, Silver, and Diamond dinners, this excessive display of wealth, privilege, and gastronomy ended up in a three-way tie.

Hotel Astor, the Plaza, the Knickerbocker, the St. Regis, Delmonico's, and Sherry's. General managers of these restaurants estimated that the amount spent on banquets during this season ranged from $500,000 to $1 million (equivalent to $15 million to $31 million today), with meals costing from $4 per plate (without extras such as wine, cigars, and entertainment) to upwards of $75 per person (including extras), which would be between $125 and $2,350 today. Some of these dinners hosted hundreds of people, with bills totaling $5,000 and more (equal to $158,000 today). The Waldorf-Astoria was particularly busy during this time, churning out hundreds of events per season, sometimes playing host to four banquets in one day totaling 2,500 people. This could include simultaneous events, with one party in the main banquet hall and another in one of the downstairs dining rooms. The number of cooks and waitstaff to pull off such a feat must have been astronomical.

Cockscombs and Other Banquet Garnishes

Theatrics were an integral part of fine dining. Lavish centerpieces, ranging from floral arrangements to ornate sugar molds and plaster-casted animals, were front and center on the banquet table. This same pageantry was often applied to the centerpiece of the meal—the main meat course. Not only was the serving plate generally well garnished, but the tops of the meat often included additional ornamentation that gave the dish increased height and grandeur. Game birds such as pheasant often included real feathers sticking out of the cooked bird or pie.

One utensil that has disappeared from our modern table is the atelette, or hatelet—a skewer generally made of silver or silver-plated metal and topped with an ornamental head. Tidbits such as vegetables, truffles, seafood, and cockscombs—the brilliant red adornments found on roosters' heads—were placed on these skewers and used to garnish both hot and cold meat dishes. The skewers "turned horizontal presentations into architectural fantasies," according to the editors of the catalogue for *Feeding Desire: Design and the Tools of the Table 1500–2005*, a 2006 exhibition at the Smithsonian's Cooper-Hewitt National Design Museum. The atelette skewer would only be used for garnishing and not for cooking. Think of it as a drink umbrella for your meat.

For additional drama, the atelettes could also be threaded with molded jellies, which would shimmer in the candle or gaslight, or whole shrimp or crawfish. The use of atelettes was popularized by French chef Urbain Dubois, author of numerous cookbooks and credited with introducing the practice of service *à la russe*—the table practice we generally use today where courses of plated food are brought to the table. His over-the-top garnishes were copied by many New York chefs during the Gilded Age.

Contributed by food historian and culinary stylist Dan Macey

Dishes featuring ornamental atelettes, Mrs. Beeton's Book of Household Management, *1923 edition* WIKIMEDIA COMMONS

Oysters on the Half Shell

Throughout the Gilded Age, a lavish meal always featured oysters as a first course, and banquet dinners were the ultimate in extravagance. Guests would have expected *oysters. Some banquet dinners even used oysters as the theme and had multiple oyster courses, each featuring a different preparation such as raw, scalloped, stewed, and fried.*

SERVES 4

24 oysters
1 lemon, cut into wedges
Chopped shallots or prepared horseradish
Salt
Pepper

Wash and shuck the oysters (or ask your fishmonger to shuck the oysters for you). Remove and discard the upper shell. Detach each oyster from the lower shell and set it back inside the shell.

Arrange 6 oysters on each of four round plates or shallow glass bowls filled with crushed ice. Place a wedge of lemon in the middle of each dish.

Put the rest of the lemon wedges in a small bowl and serve oysters with the extra lemon, a dish of chopped shallots or horseradish, and salt and pepper.

Pot-au-Feu

Literally translated as "pot on the fire," pot-au-feu is a thick, hearty beef stew that is often called the national dish of France. This version is adapted from a nineteenth-century recipe taught by French chef Pierre Blot at the launch of his New York Cooking Academy in 1865. Blot called this stew's rich broth the "foundation upon which good cooking is based." In French cooking, it is often used as a base for other soups or stews, or to flavor dishes such as fricandeau of veal.

SERVES 6–8

6 pounds fresh beef (ribs, knuckle, or loin cut)

Salt and pepper

2 white onions, peeled

2 whole cloves

1 parsnip, peeled and chopped into 2-inch pieces

4 carrots, peeled and chopped into 2-inch pieces

6 celery stalks, chopped into 2-inch pieces

2 turnips, peeled and quartered

2 leeks, white and pale green parts only, thinly sliced

2 sprigs fresh parsley

1 sprig fresh thyme

1 garlic clove, peeled

1 teaspoon whole peppercorns

2 teaspoons coarse salt

1 bay leaf

Dijon mustard, horseradish, coarse salt, and/or cornichons for serving

Season the beef with salt and pepper and place in a large pot or Dutch oven with 5 quarts of cold water. Simmer over low heat for 2 hours, skimming off any foam that rises to the surface.

Stick a clove into each of the two onions and place in a cheesecloth bag along with parsnip, carrots, celery, turnips, leeks, parsley, thyme, garlic, peppercorns, salt, and bay leaf. Add to the pot with the beef and continue to simmer for 2–3 hours or until meat is tender.

Remove the meat and place on a large cutting board. Cut into 2-inch pieces and place in a large serving bowl.

Pot-au-Feu

CONTINUED

Take the vegetables out of the cheesecloth bag. Remove the cloves from the onions and discard. Chop the onions into thick slices and add to the serving bowl along with the parsnip, carrots, celery, turnips, and leeks. Discard the parsley, thyme, garlic, peppercorns, and bay leaf. Cover the bowl with aluminum foil to keep warm and set aside.

Strain the broth through a fine sieve into a large bowl. Pour the broth back into the soup pot and cook over medium-high heat until boiling. Take off the heat, skim off any remaining surface fat, and then pour some broth over the meat and vegetables in the serving bowl. Serve with little dishes of Dijon mustard, horseradish, coarse salt, and/or cornichons.

NOTE: *The remaining broth can be kept in the refrigerator for a few days or frozen for future use.*

Chicken Salad

Chicken salad was a such a staple dish for Gilded Age banquets and lunches that place settings at these events often included a separate fork specifically for it. The recipe below is adapted from Philadelphia cooking school instructor Sarah Tyson Rorer, who stipulated the chicken should be "especially boiled for salad and carefully seasoned while boiling." Her recipe says to use a whole chicken, but I have updated it to use boneless chicken breasts, which is much easier. Taking the step to boil the chicken with the aromatics adds a flavorful layer of depth to the meat.

SERVES 4

1 (1½-pound) package boneless chicken breasts
1 small carrot
½ teaspoon whole peppercorns
½ onion
1 bay leaf
¼ teaspoon celery seed
1 teaspoon lemon juice
½ teaspoon salt
¼ teaspoon paprika
½ cup chopped celery
½ cup mayonnaise (or to taste), either homemade (see page 113) or jarred
Green or red leaf lettuce, celery tips, and olives for garnish

Place chicken, carrot, peppercorns, onion, bay leaf, and celery seed in a large pot over medium-high heat. Add water to cover. Bring to a boil, then cover pot and reduce heat to medium-low. Simmer until chicken is cooked through, about 10 minutes.

Using a large fork or tongs, remove the chicken from the pot and place in a colander to cool. Discard cooking water and aromatics.

Dice chicken into 1-inch pieces. Place in a large bowl and toss with lemon juice, salt, and paprika, then add celery and mayonnaise. Mix well and chill until ready to serve.

To serve, line a salad bowl with lettuce leaves. Add the chicken salad and garnish with celery tips and olives if desired.

Chocolate Jelly

In the nineteenth century, gelatin, or "jelly" as it was often called, was created by making a thick stock from animal products rich in natural gelatin. Peter Cooper (who also invented the steam locomotive) took the first steps in making this lengthy process much easier by receiving the first US patent for a gelatin dessert powder in 1845. Even though this must have been a huge time-saver, it wasn't until Charles Knox introduced granulated gelatin in 1894 that the idea really took off and the brand became somewhat of a household word. Kraft Foods' Jell-O came soon after, created by a carpenter named Pearle Wait in 1897. This allowed popular gelatin desserts to come together much quicker and easier.

SERVES 6–8

2 packets unflavored gelatin (like Knox)

4 ounces (1 package) unsweetened baking chocolate

2 cups milk

1 tablespoon vanilla extract

½ cup sugar

Mint sprigs, for garnish (optional)

Whipped cream, for serving (optional)

Place ½ cup cold water in a small mixing bowl. Sprinkle gelatin over top, stirring to dissolve. Let stand for 1 minute, then add ½ cup boiling water, stirring constantly until gelatin is completely dissolved.

Break up chocolate into small squares and place in a glass dish. Microwave on high in 30-second intervals, stirring in between until melted. Let cool briefly.

While chocolate is cooling, heat milk in a medium saucepan over medium-low heat until small bubbles begin to form around the edges, about 2 minutes. Remove from heat and add chocolate, vanilla, sugar, and gelatin. Stir to combine.

Spray a 4-cup mold (the one I use is 6 x 6 inches) with cooking spray. Pour the jelly mixture into the mold and place in the refrigerator until set, at least 6 hours or overnight.

When ready to unmold, place a serving plate over the bottom of the mold and flip it over. If the jelly is not coming out easily, you can try placing the mold in a bowl of warm water (being careful not to fully submerge) for about 10 seconds. Then carefully run a sharp knife around the edge of the mold to loosen. Garnish with mint sprigs if desired and serve with fresh whipped cream (see recipe on page 83).

BALLS

Alva Vanderbilt, Vanderbilt Costume Ball, 1883 WIKIMEDIA COMMONS

Gilded Age balls were grand events that showed off wealth, privilege, and power within one's social circle. Many were themed to coincide with a particular event or time of the year. For example, debutante balls were a way to introduce young ladies into society so they could find suitable husbands. Charity balls were a way to raise funds for specific causes, such as the Turkish Ball given at the New York Academy of Music in 1877 to raise money for those wounded in the Russian-Turkish war. Others were simply a way to socialize and flaunt status, such as the Patriarch Balls created by Ward McAllister, whose twenty-five exclusive members rotated hosting duties.

McAllister was recruited by Caroline Astor, considered the most influential of New York's social sphere, to make sure this group remained limited to her old-money contemporaries. The magnificent ball she hosted in her Fifth Avenue

Debutante Balls

Young ladies would make their "debut into society" at private balls given by their parents. The debutante would wear a white dress made from satin, silk, surah, crepe-de-chine, or foulard fabric. White shoes, stockings, and gloves completed the look, with the virtuous white color representing the lady's young age and the occasion of her first dance in public. When supper was announced, the debutante's father would escort her to the table with her mother entering last, accompanied by the gentleman she wanted to honor for the evening. The debutante's partner for her first dance was typically a young man who was a family member or close friend, selected by her mother. Balls could take place at the home of the young lady or a restaurant such as Delmonico's, host to many debutante balls during the Gilded Age.

Bradley-Martin Ball

Gilded Age society loved to one-up each other by hosting affairs that were increasingly over the top. Although Ward McAllister was the era's most prolific social organizer, there were others who played host to sensational events, often as a way to muscle their way to the top of the list of the "Four Hundred." One of these was the Bradley-Martin costume ball, hosted by Cornelia Bradley-Martin, wife of socialite Bradley Martin, at the Waldorf-Astoria in 1897. Guests were instructed to come dressed as European royalty of old, with Cornelia's hope that these costume purchases and other preparations would help boost the economy, which was still flagging following the Panic of 1893. Many guests rented rooms at the Waldorf and hired private hairdressers and maids to help them get dressed in their intricate costumes. The cost of the ball was in the hundreds of thousands, comparable to about $10 million today.

The event's breathtaking flowers were sent from hothouses all over the Northeast, including Albany and Rochester, New York, as well as Washington, DC, and South Carolina. A canopy of pink and white roses accented by green galax leaves framed the small ballroom where Mrs. Bradley-Martin received her guests. Supper was served at 1:00 a.m. in the Winter Garden, where deep pink American Beauty and yellow roses were intertwined with sprays of white mimosa, piled high around the one hundred small tables. The multi-course meal featured twenty-five different dishes, including consommé, lobster Newburg, filet of beef, chicken stuffed with truffles, foie gras, game birds, fruit gelée with whipped cream, cakes, biscuits, sorbets, ices, petits fours, and bonbons, accompanied by expensive Moet & Chandon Brut Imperial Champagne and Bordeaux from France's Château Mouton-d'Armailhacq. Twelve hundred invitations were sent out, but only a little more than half that amount attended. The *New York Times* speculated that many guests came strictly out of curiosity to see the decorations and their fellow guests' costumes, especially since many left the ball even before the dancing began.

Supper Buffet for a Ball or Reception, Mrs. Beeton's Book of Household Management, *1907*

mansion every January was the highlight of the social season. Those on the guest list were members of the "Four Hundred," a select list of the only people she and McAllister deemed socially worthy. They had allegedly determined four hundred was the limit, as that was how many people could comfortably fit in her huge ballroom. But over the years there was some debate about the group's origins. For example, a *New York Tribune* article from 1889 called it the "sheerest nonsense," stating it wasn't Ward McAllister who created the Four Hundred, but rather Charles Delmonico when he built a hall that would hold just that number of people. In any case, parties and balls for this exclusive group continued throughout the Gilded Age. And Mrs. Astor did relent in 1883, allowing the Vanderbilts (with their new money funded by the railroads) into the fold so that her daughter Carrie could attend Alva Vanderbilt's extravagant masquerade ball. Soon other families trickled in as well.

Balls and other types of dancing parties were such an important part of Gilded Age society that the etiquette of balls and the ballroom were integral to the "training of well-bred young people." The hostess giving the ball needed to provide a pleasant and entertaining evening for her guests. Not only would guests discuss the ball afterward among themselves, but these types of society events were often written up in local newspapers. As noted in the 1890 book

Mr. Bennett's Domino Ball

Newport, Rhode Island, was the site of many Gilded Age balls, including a Domino Ball in September 1884. Domino Balls were a throwback to eighteenth-century masquerade balls where one of the costumes was a domino in the form of a large cloak that covered the entire body, sometimes with a hood. Given by James Gordon Bennett Jr., publisher of the *New York Herald* (and son of founder James Gordon Bennett Sr.), the seven-hundred-person guest list included notables such as President Chester Arthur, Attorney General Benjamin Brewster, and members of the Buffalo polo team. The ball included an elaborate supper and a German dance (a ballroom dance also called a cotillon) for seventy couples. But the highlight of the evening was a quadrille featuring nine couples, with the men disguised in animal and bird masks and the ladies dressed in domino costumes. The *New York Times* estimated the entire night cost at least $6,000, about $188,000 today.

Modern Manners and Social Forms, a successful ball required "a well-bred hostess, good ventilation, good music, a good supper, guests who know their duties, and not too large a number of them." Following proper protocol was necessary for every detail, from the invitations, preparations, and music to the receiving of the guests, supper, and refreshments. The number of guests could range from one hundred to seven hundred or more.

Food at balls was bountiful. Refreshments included oysters, turkey, chicken, grouse, canvasback duck, terrapin, turtle, cold salmon, salads of all types, oyster and game patties, biscuits, jellies, creams, fruits, bonbons, and ices, all accompanied by a variety of wines. These dishes were typically placed on a buffet or side table and served throughout the evening. The table was elegantly decorated with fresh fruit and flowers and the food served on the finest cut-glass, china, and silverware. In addition, sometimes the hostess would serve a more formal supper at midnight. The host would lead the way to the dining room with the most distinguished lady guest on his arm, and the hostess would enter last, making sure all was in order in the ballroom.

Mrs. Vanderbilt's Decorated Dishes

The ball given by Mrs. Cornelius Vanderbilt in 1888 in her new home on New York's West 57th Street was magnificent in every way, but especially over the top in its food presentation. Her culinary experts worked for months planning and preparing the food, which included several extremely detailed dishes. These types of artistic arrangements were popular additions to Gilded Age tables. Chefs would mold food into intricate forms and then embellish them with fashionable garnishes, which included decorative molds made from cold cooked foods set in aspic (a savory, transparent gelatin). The jelly encasing the cooked meat looked pretty and prevented air and bacteria from turning the meat rancid. The result was an attractive display, like museum pieces under glass.

1 WEST 57TH STREET.

LE 23 JANVIER, 1888.

Chaud

Consommé en tasse — Huîtres à la poulette
Croquettes de volaille — Bouchées à la reine
Térrapène à la Maryland — Canvas-back duck

Froid

Galantine de chapon — Filet de boeuf, jardinière
Aspic de foie-gras, Belle-vue
Chaufroid de mauviette — Pâté de gibier, chasseur
Pâté de Strasbourg, naturel
Saumon à la Vatel — Jambon à la gelée
Salade de poulet — Salade de homard
Volière de cailles — Sandwiches variés

Entremets

Charlotte moderne
Gelée macédoine aux fruits — Glaces assorties
Dessert

Vanderbilt Ball Menu, 1888 NEW YORK PUBLIC LIBRARY

The dishes at Mrs. Vanderbilt's ball represented scenes from nature and Roman mythology, such as a pheasant game pie held up by deer's antlers, with two rabbits playing cards underneath. A filet of beef garnished with vegetables rested on the shoulders of Hercules, accompanied by wax cupids. The god Mercury was poised in flight over a piece of ham decorated with truffles. But a pool of water containing real fish, tadpoles, and frogs held the most striking display: a two-foot-long salmon nestled in a wax boat, pulled by Neptune driving a sea horse–led chariot made from seashells. At midnight a full menu was served featuring hot dishes such as consommé en tasse (tiny cups of clear consommé), bouchees à la reine (puff pastry with chicken in a Madeira sauce), and terrapene à la Maryland (terrapin in a sherry sauce), as well as several cold dishes such as galantine de chapon (boned and stuffed capon), filet de boeuf, jardinière (filet of beef garnished with vegetables), and jambon à la gelée (jellied ham). Desserts included charlotte moderne, gelée macédoine aux fruits (fruit jelly), and glacés assorties (assorted ices).

Lobster Fricassee

A fricassee is a kind of stew featuring chicken, veal, lamb, or fish that is first sautéed or fried, then smothered in a thickened white or brown stock. This cooking method was very popular in the nineteenth century, often as a way to tenderize tougher cuts of meat. However, this recipe, adapted from Eliza Leslie's mid-century cookbook Directions for Cookery, *calls for lobster, a dinner-party fixture on the tables of the über-wealthy and influential during the Gilded Age. Feel free to substitute shrimp or clams for the lobster if you wish.*

 **SERVES 2 AS A MAIN DISH OR 4 AS AN APPETIZER** 

4 frozen puff pastry shells (like Pepperidge Farm)
1 teaspoon salt, divided
2 large lobster tails
½ teaspoon cayenne pepper
½ teaspoon ground nutmeg
1 cup heavy cream
1 egg yolk, beaten
Fresh parsley sprigs for garnish, optional

Preheat oven to 400°F.

Set puff pastry shells on an ungreased baking sheet with top side facing up. Place in the oven on the middle rack and bake for 20–25 minutes.

While pastry is baking, fill a large pot with water. Add ½ teaspoon salt and bring to a boil. Add the lobster tails and boil for 2–3 minutes. (You want to just parboil the tails since they will continue to cook when fricasseed.)

Carefully remove the tails to a large cutting board with a pair of tongs. Drain water from the pot, straining some through a fine sieve into a 1-cup measure for later.

Extract the lobster meat from the shells, chopping it into small pieces. Place the lobster meat in a medium bowl and season with cayenne, nutmeg, and ½ teaspoon salt.

Transfer lobster meat to a large saucepan set over medium heat and slowly add the cream and ½ cup of reserved lobster stock. Cook for about 5 minutes, stirring occasionally. Do not allow to boil. Stir in the beaten egg yolk and cook for 1–2 minutes, stirring to combine. If sauce is too thick, add a little more lobster stock to thin it out.

When pastry shells are done (they should be a golden brown color), remove from the oven. Cool for 1–2 minutes and then scoop off the top and soft pastry underneath with a fork. Fill shells with lobster mixture, then garnish with fresh parsley if desired. Serve immediately.

Charlotte Russe

In the nineteenth century it was fashionable to name foods after famous people. These dishes were either a favorite of that person or created in their honor, as is the case with charlotte russe, which was technically named after two people. "Charlotte" desserts originated in England at the end of the eighteenth century and are essentially puddings poured into a mold that has been lined with bread or sponge fingers. The name is thought to be in honor of Queen Charlotte, the wife of George III of England. Charlotte russe came a few years later. A luscious, chilled dessert of vanilla Bavarian cream set in a mold lined with ladyfingers, it was created by French chef Carême at the beginning of the nineteenth century. Carême originally called the dish Charlotte à la Parisienne, but it is believed he changed it to charlotte russe in honor of Russian Tsar Alexander I. This Gilded Age staple embraced the use of boxed gelatin, a culinary innovation at the time.

SERVES 10–12

2 packets unflavored gelatin (such as Knox)

3 large eggs

½ cup sugar

¼ teaspoon salt

2 cups milk

1 tablespoon vanilla extract, plus 1 teaspoon

3 cups heavy cream

½ cup confectioners' sugar

2 (3-ounce) packages soft ladyfingers

1 pint fresh strawberries (or other fruit)

Place a metal mixing bowl and beater(s) from an electric mixer in the freezer.

In a medium mixing bowl, sprinkle unflavored gelatin over ½ cup cold water. Let stand for 1 minute, then add ½ cup boiling water, stirring constantly until granules are completely dissolved.

Combine eggs, sugar, and salt in a large bowl. Stir well with a whisk.

Heat milk in a large, heavy saucepan over medium-high heat until tiny bubbles form around the edge (do not boil). Turn heat to low and gradually add the egg mixture, stirring constantly with a whisk for about 3–4 minutes or until thickened. Stir in 1 tablespoon vanilla.

Charlotte Russe

Pour the milk mixture into the gelatin in the mixing bowl and let cool for 20 minutes, stirring occasionally.

Remove the chilled bowl and beater(s) from freezer. Place cream, confectioners' sugar, and 1 teaspoon vanilla in the bowl and whip with an electric mixer on medium speed for about 5–7 minutes or until firm peaks form. Set aside 1 cup for topping.

Grease a springform pan (or spray with cooking spray) and then line the bottom and sides with ladyfingers, using whipped cream to "glue" them together to form a solid base.

Fold the remaining whipped cream minus the reserved 1 cup into the custard mixture and then pour over ladyfingers. Place in the freezer for 1 hour and then take out and carefully unmold onto a plate.

Refrigerate until ready to serve. Just prior to serving, top with the reserved whipped cream and garnish with strawberries or other fruit.

Chilled Green Bean Salad

According to nineteenth-century cookbook author Maria Parloa, "There is hardly a vegetable which is not used, either cooked or raw, in salad." The same holds true today, and green beans are no exception. If you have the time, French-cut the beans as suggested by this adapted version from Mary Henderson's 1878 cookbook, Practical Cooking and Dinner Giving, *as it makes a lovely presentation. You can also cut the beans using the slicing blade of your food processor. If you can't find tarragon vinegar, substitute white wine vinegar and add ½ teaspoon dried tarragon to the marinade.*

SERVES 4

1 pound fresh green beans, trimmed

FOR THE MARINADE:

3 tablespoons tarragon vinegar

1 tablespoon olive oil

⅛ teaspoon salt

⅛ teaspoon pepper

FOR THE FRENCH DRESSING:

⅛ teaspoon salt

⅛ teaspoon pepper

3 tablespoons olive oil

1 tablespoon tarragon vinegar

1 teaspoon Dijon mustard

To make the marinade, combine vinegar, olive oil, salt, and pepper in a small bowl. Stir with a whisk. Set aside.

To make the dressing, place salt, pepper, and one tablespoon oil in a small bowl. Stir with a whisk, then alternately add the rest of the oil, vinegar, and mustard, whisking well. Set aside.

Have ready a large bowl of ice water. Cut the green beans on a diagonal and then slice each in half lengthwise to make two thin slices.

Bring 6–8 quarts of water to a rolling boil in a large stockpot over medium-high heat. Add the green beans and cover the pot. When the water comes back to a boil, uncover and continue cooking for 5–8 minutes or until the beans are crisp-tender. Remove the beans with a large slotted spoon and immediately place in the bowl of ice water to stop the cooking process. Drain in a colander.

When cool, arrange the green beans on a platter or shallow dish. Season with the marinade and refrigerate. When ready to serve, drain the marinade and mix the green beans with French dressing to taste, placing any remaining dressing in a pitcher to serve at the table.

CHAPTER FOUR
BY INVITATION ONLY

To give a luncheon is to indulge one's self in the most charming and satisfying form of entertainment.

—MRS. CAROLINE BENEDICT BURRELL, AUTHOR OF *GALA DAY LUNCHEONS: A LITTLE BOOK OF SUGGESTIONS* FOR CELEBRATORY LUNCH PARTIES FIRST PUBLISHED IN 1901

FORMAL SOCIAL OCCASIONS were an integral part of the Gilded Age—a way to meet with friends and acquaintances, form new connections, arrange plans for future get-togethers, and pay off social obligations. Specific protocols were required, from fancy, engraved invitations to clothing, menu, and table service. This chapter features typical recipes from these types of entertainments.

DINNER PARTIES

During the Gilded Age, prosperous Americans went out of their way to make sure others were aware of their wealth and status, consuming goods on a level that was unprecedented. This included investments in items such as enormous mansions, fancy carriages, rare paintings, luxurious clothing, and plush furnishings. Another way they liked to "show off" their excess wealth was by hosting social events in their homes, including elaborate dinner parties. These exclusive gatherings helped tighten the society circles of old money and traditional American bloodlines, although families with newer fortunes built on the era's technological advances, such as the Vanderbilts, eventually broke through this barrier.

In order to pull off extravagant dinner parties successfully, many of the über-rich hired private French chefs, a concept kicked off by banker and diplomat August Belmont in 1857. These chefs soon became an upper-class fixture, with society women such as Marietta Stevens (the wife of hotelier Paran Stevens) paying reputable French chefs upwards of $45 a week (equal to about $1,200 today) to do their personal cooking. For those who did not employ

Residence of Mrs. Paran Stevens, New York City, 1894 LIBRARY OF CONGRESS

Outrageous Dinner Parties with Animal Guests

By the turn of the twentieth century, unusually themed dinner parties became all the rage. Mamie Fish, wife of railroad magnate Stuyvesant Fish, and Harry Lehr, husband of New York socialite Elizabeth Wharton Drexel, particularly enjoyed the shock value of planning and hosting outrageous dinners. This included a dogs' dinner, where society pets were served a three-course banquet at their own table. Mrs. Fish even bought her dog a $15,000 diamond collar for the occasion. They then made a monkey the guest of honor at a Newport dinner given by the Lehrs in 1902. Mrs. Fish met the monkey, named Jocko, on board a yacht she rode from New York to Newport and thought it would be amusing to dress him up and bring him to the Lehrs' dinner party. She had a tailor make him a miniature suit featuring red trousers with black trim and a little jacket with a tiny watch chain, which had to be removed as he kept wanting to eat it.

Mrs. Fish asked the Lehrs if she could bring a guest along, not specifying the guest was really a monkey. When they arrived, the hosts were amused and went along with the joke. They had saved the head of the table for Mrs. Fish's distinguished visitor, who proceeded to dine with the other guests. All was merry until Jocko was given liquor to drink and then proceeded to throw glasses and plates at the other guests, causing the women to run from the table—and the event to garner some bad press. As a result, some of the guests and the Lehrs later denied it, with Harry telling the *New York Times*, "That monkey story is a wicked falsehood and malicious slander."

a chef, Gilded Age society authority Ward McAllister recommended knowing an "artist" that could be hired for special occasions.

Although dinner party menus varied, there was a kind of "standard" that was followed regarding the course themes. They typically began with raw oysters and Champagne, followed by a choice of clear or brown soup (such as consommé or green turtle), served with sherry. Fish was the third course, often paired with Chablis, then an entrée such as asparagus with mousseline sauce or carrots and turnips à la poulette (literally translated as "entrance" or "beginning," entrées were meant to show off the skill and artistry of the chef, not serve as the main dish as they often do today). The roast (some kind of meat or poultry) was next, served with claret and Champagne, then a palate-cleansing punch or sorbet. Next was game (such as snipe or canvasback duck) with Madeira and port, followed by a course of salad or cold dishes, then a cheese course. Dessert was also served in several separate courses, including pastry or pudding, ices and ice creams, fresh fruit with sherry or claret, and finally nuts and dried fruit. At the end of the meal, ladies retired to the drawing room (living room) for black coffee, bonbons, and brandy, while the men either remained at the table to enjoy cigars, liquors, and small talk or moved to the library, eventually joining the women in the drawing room before finally calling it a night.

Fish Dishes, Mrs. Beeton's Book of Household Management, *1923 edition* WIKIMEDIA COMMONS

Fancy Cakes, Mrs. Beeton's Book of Household Management, *1923 edition* WIKIMEDIA COMMONS

Salmon en Papillotes

Cooking items in little bundles of parchment or foil is not only neat and practical, but also makes a very pretty presentation. We can thank the French for popularizing the technique, called en papillote, *which arose from the classic French haute cuisine of the eighteenth century. Perfect for a dinner party, it allows guests to each open their own individual package. It also ensures the salmon is cooked perfectly, a fact that Gilded Age cooking expert Pierre Blot admitted was "very difficult, if not nearly impossible."*

SERVES 4

¼ cup minced fresh parsley
½ teaspoon salt
¼ teaspoon pepper
1 tablespoon unsalted butter, melted
⅛ teaspoon ground nutmeg
Zest and juice from 1 lemon
4 (6–8 ounce) salmon fillets

Preheat oven to 400°F.

Mix parsley, salt, pepper, butter, nutmeg, and lemon juice and zest together in a small bowl.

Cut four pieces of parchment paper into rectangles about 8 x 5 inches in size. Lightly grease each piece of parchment paper with a little olive oil, butter, or cooking spray.

Place each piece of fish onto one of the parchment pieces. Top each with a spoonful of the parsley-lemon mixture, dividing evenly among the four pieces. Fold the wider ends of the paper over the fillets and then fold the two shorter edges together, crimping so it forms a tightly sealed package.

Place on a baking sheet and bake for 10–15 minutes. The parchment packages should puff up into attractive bundles. To serve, cut crosswise slits in the paper to release the steam.

Game Dishes, Mrs. Beeton's Book of Household Management, *1923 edition* WIKIMEDIA COMMONS

Pommes de Terre à la Brabant

Brabant potatoes are diced fried potatoes with parsley and butter. The potatoes are parboiled, then finished off in a frying pan, resulting in potatoes that are delightfully tender and fluffy on the inside and crispy on the outside. A popular side dish in New Orleans today, they were often served with the poisson *(fish) course at dinner parties during the Gilded Age.*

2 pounds yellow or Yukon Gold potatoes

3 tablespoons canola oil

2 tablespoons chopped fresh parsley

1 teaspoon salt

½ teaspoon pepper

Juice of 1 lemon

2 tablespoons unsalted butter

Peel potatoes and cut into 1-inch dice. Place in a medium pot and cover with water. Bring water to a boil and cook for about 5 minutes or until potatoes yield slightly with a fork. Drain potatoes in a colander.

Heat oil in a heavy skillet over medium-high heat. Add potatoes and cook for about 10 minutes until light brown and crisp, turning occasionally to brown on all sides. Add the parsley, salt, pepper, and lemon juice and stir for about 1 minute to coat. Add the butter and stir until melted. Remove to a serving bowl and serve immediately.

Betteraves Nouvelles au Beurre

This dish is literally translated as "buttered new beets." These would have been tender, early-harvest beets, grown in southern states and shipped to markets in the Northeast starting in the beginning of June. To best replicate what would have been served in the Gilded Age, try to get small baby beets for this recipe if you can. Leaving the two ends intact while cooking helps prevent the beets from "bleeding."

SERVES 4

1 pound (about 5 small or 3–4 medium) beets
1 tablespoon unsalted butter
½ teaspoon salt
¼ teaspoon pepper

Scrub beets to remove any dirt. Trim the roots and stems so that 1 inch remains. Place in a medium pot, then add water to cover and bring to a boil. Once water is boiling, turn down to low and simmer for 20–30 minutes or until desired tenderness.

Have ready a bowl of cold water. Drain beets and place in the cold water. Slip off the skin and cut the beets in thin slices or small dice.

Melt the butter and combine with the salt and pepper. Pour over the beets and stir to coat. Serve immediately.

Chocolate Biscuits

These delightful biscuits are adapted from French chef Pierre Blot's 1863 cookbook, What to Eat, and How to Cook It. *They are very similar to Savoy biscuits, which originated in France in the 1600s. Similar to a sponge cake, Savoy biscuits call for beating the eggs separately. First the egg yolks are beaten with the sugar, then the flour is added, and at the end, foamy egg whites are folded in, helping create lovely pockets of air bubbles in the batter, resulting in a light, delicate biscuit. Sometimes a flavoring was added such as cinnamon, lemon, orange, vanilla, or even chocolate, as in this version.*

6 large eggs, separated
1 cup sugar
1½ cups all-purpose flour
2 ounces (½ package) baking chocolate, grated
½ cup bittersweet chocolate chips

Preheat oven to 350°F.

Beat the egg yolks and sugar together in a large bowl on medium-high speed for about 2–3 minutes until a pale yellow color. Slowly add the flour and grated chocolate and mix well.

In a separate glass or stainless steel bowl, beat the egg whites on medium until soft peaks form, about 3–4 minutes. Gently fold into chocolate mixture.

Spoon the batter into mini cupcake pans or molds lined with baking papers. Bake for 10–12 minutes and then remove to a wire rack.

When the biscuits have cooled, place the chocolate chips in a glass bowl. Microwave on high in 30-second intervals, stirring in between until melted. Dip the biscuits into the melted chocolate or spread chocolate carefully over the biscuits. Allow to cool thoroughly before serving—the chocolate will harden and form a nice glaze.

LADIES' LUNCHEONS

Lunches and luncheons were two distinctly different events during the Gilded Age. A lunch was more informal, a meal enjoyed by just the members of a household in the middle of the day. A luncheon, however, was much grander. Held after breakfast and before the evening dinner hour, it was considered a form of entertainment and would often feature a performance by a young actor, vocalist, or public speaker. According to the 1896 book *Social Etiquette*, these events rapidly gained in popularity in the late 1800s and were "more frequently extended to ladies alone . . . given by a woman to women."

Luncheon Salads, Mrs. Beeton's Book of Household Management, *1923 edition*

The menu could be quite extensive, with a mix of hot and cold foods such as cream of asparagus soup, oysters, salads, small game, lamb chops with green peas and potatoes, hot rolls, fancy cakes, ices, hot chocolate, and "a variety of dishes which will destroy the appetite for dinner." Or it could be simpler, consisting of cold dishes such as boned turkey, ham, raw oysters, tongue, fruit, thin-sliced bread and butter, Bavarian cream, cakes, and hot coffee. The most extravagant luncheons were those given in honor of a distinguished guest or for a special occasion, such as a bridal engagement. These would feature broiled delicacies such as fish and poultry, creamed potatoes, salads, oysters, croquettes, cup custards, fancy cakes, ices, and hot chocolate with whipped

Club Luncheons

Women's associations dedicated to various interests or activities thrived during the Gilded Age. Many were rather progressive for their time, including the Sedgeley Club (a Philadelphia women's bike, barge, and canoe club), the Topic Club (a Philadelphia literary club), Phalo (a New York club devoted to philosophic discussions), and Sorosis (a New York professional women's club). These groups often hosted "club luncheons," which followed a specific protocol of their own. They could be held in a private home, an off-site location where the club regularly met, or a hotel or restaurant. The club's president, board members, and any honored guests would form a receiving line to greet members as they arrived, then all would walk into the dining room for the luncheon, led by the president and most distinguished guest. The menu could include items such as bouillon, creamed oysters, oyster patties, chicken croquettes, salads, iced pineapple, soft-shell crabs with brown butter, broiled lamb chops, new potatoes in cream, asparagus in hollandaise sauce, Bar-le-Duc jelly and crackers, fancy creams, cakes, and coffee. Once the final course was finished, the president would call the group to order and start the program of the day, which could involve speeches, discussion, or instrumental or vocal performances.

cream, all served in separate courses. If wine was offered, it was typically only a light variety, along with mineral and still water. Strong black coffee in demitasse cups would be served as a final course at the table, rather than in the drawing room as was customary at a dinner party.

But no matter what type of food was offered, it was important for the hostess to provide the same level of exquisite taste and table décor as was expected at a dinner or banquet. This included placing artistically arranged flowers throughout the parlor and dining room. A centerpiece of fruit and flowers would be displayed on the main dining table, surrounded by glass dishes containing fancy cakes and bonbons. Petite cut-glass or silver dishes of salted

Standing Luncheons

Standing luncheons started to become popular in the 1890s. Like a less formal evening reception, they were similar to what we would think of today as an open house. They included both men and women and were often given during the busy social season preceding more formal balls or dinners held in the evening. Other times they could be a way to formally introduce a young lady to society, held prior to her debutante ball, which would take place at a later date. Although more informal than a seated luncheon, they still featured numerous floral arrangements and other fashionable décor.

After being greeted by the host and hostess in the reception (living) room, guests would move into the dining room, where they could remain standing or seat themselves in chairs or sofas placed around the sides of the room, served by waiters or their escorts. The serving table featured a variety of hot and cold dishes "that could be eaten easily with a fork or spoon" and piles of plates, napkins, and silverware situated in easy reach. The beverage service was laid out on the sideboard, including light wines, punch, cups for coffee and hot chocolate, wineglasses, goblets, and tumblers for ice water. The first course was typically cups of bouillon, followed by small plates of creamed oysters and bite-size delicacies such as lobster croquettes or mushroom pâté. The third course would be chicken croquettes or rissoles (tiny pastry-wrapped meat patties), a lettuce or celery salad, and petite sandwiches made from potted meat, sardines, or lobster mayonnaise. The final sweets course would feature molded ice creams, biscuits, and fancy cakes, followed by coffee or hot chocolate.

almonds and olives were scattered around the table. A single rose and fancy name cards were often placed by each place setting, as well as party favors such as satin bags filled with confectionery, tiny flower baskets, hand-painted book covers, or Japanese fans. The dining room was often darkened by drawing the shades, lit with wax candles for soft, ambient lighting.

Sometimes luncheons followed a specific theme; for example, a "Blue and White Tableware" luncheon, where the table decorations were all shades of blue and white, from bluet and marguerite flowers and linens accented with blue embroidery to delft-style china and a blue and white candelabra. Or a "Betrothal Luncheon" to celebrate an engagement, featuring rose-hued food and décor, such as a wreath of paper roses encircling the chandelier, sorbet molded in the shape of pink roses, cupid figurines holding dishes of candied rose leaves, and heart-shaped cakes with pink icing. For these events it was customary for a ring to be baked into the cake, with the belief that the young lady who received that piece would be the next to be married.

Luncheons at a country house were often served on little tables outside, sometimes as a progressive meal, with guests changing seats each time a new course was brought out. The menu was less formal for these occasions, featuring food such as curried chicken, rice and bananas, and omelette soufflé.

Ebenezer Maxwell Mansion, Philadelphia, Pennsylvania

When Lobster Got Fancy

Many Gilded Age meals included a fish course that often featured some type of lobster dish. However, lobsters were just beginning to gain in popularity as a status symbol, as they were once considered food for the poor.

Lobsters, most famously native to the Maine coast, were so plentiful to Native Americans and early European settlers that they were used as fish bait and fertilizer. Residents of the Massachusetts Bay Colony found them washed up on shore sometimes in two-foot-high piles. In 1622, William Bradford, the governor of the Plymouth Colony, was reluctant to tell newly arriving Pilgrims that unfortunately the only food he could offer them was lobsters, not even bread. Their abundance meant that they were easily accessed by all, and they garnered a reputation as a poor man's food. They were fed to prisoners, apprentices, and the enslaved as a way to save money.

But all that changed mostly because of two things—canning and the railroads. With canned food now available, people outside of New England could purchase cheap canned lobster, which became one of the most popular canned products on the market. Maine had multiple canneries in the early 1800s, processing lobsters much larger than today, with five pounds considered small. The lobster at the time was cooked dead and then canned. The onset of the Civil War made canning a viable way of getting food rations to thousands of troops. Lobster was described by one historian as "cheap and high in protein, basically chewable fuel."

When railroads began serving canned lobster to their guests, the crustacean's availability started to drop. Passengers generally found the lobster exotic and began asking for it after dining by rail. As they began to travel and take trips to New England to try fresh lobster, demand increased in other parts of the country. In the 1850s and 1860s, lobster was served most often as a salad or condiment. Whole lobsters began appearing as part of fancy centerpieces due to their exotic and interesting appearance. By the 1880s, chefs discovered lobster tasted better if they cooked it live. The lobster's association with wealth and status peaked during the Gilded Age when even Diamond Jim Brady, the country's foremost gourmet at the time, was seen eating six or seven lobsters at one seating.

Contributed by food historian and culinary stylist Dan Macey

Escarole Salad

This recipe is adapted from the 1885 cookbook Fifty Salads *by Thomas Jefferson Murrey, who had served as professional caterer of the Astor House in New York and the Continental Hotel in Philadelphia. In the book's introduction, Murrey refers to salads as "the Prince of the Menu," stating that an "affair will be voted a failure if that be poor." He describes this escarole salad recipe as "one of the best salads known." A piece of garlic-rubbed crust (known as the* chapon*) is added to the salad to impart flavor and then removed prior to serving.*

1 large head escarole lettuce, washed, dried, and torn into bite-size pieces

1 garlic clove, peeled

1 teaspoon salt, divided

1 crust day-old bread

¼ teaspoon pepper

¼ cup extra-virgin olive oil

1 tablespoon tarragon or white wine vinegar

Place the escarole in a large salad bowl.

Place the garlic glove on a cutting board and crush with the flat side of a chef's knife to release the flavor. Dip the crushed garlic in ½ teaspoon salt and then rub it all over the crust of bread. Add the crust to the salad bowl with the escarole.

Make the dressing by combining ½ teaspoon salt, pepper, olive oil, and vinegar in a glass jar. Shake well and pour over escarole. Toss the leaves with the dressing so they are well coated. Remove the bread crust and serve immediately.

Lobster Salad

Lobster salads were one of the most frequently featured salads on luncheon menus during the Gilded Age. As a 1901 issue of Domestic Science Monthly *proclaimed, "Luncheon salads should be rich, meaty and sufficient. Fish salads are better at lunch than at dinner. Lobster salad stands first." Many lobster salads from the era call for marinating the lobster first with French dressing prior to adding the mayonnaise, as is the case with this recipe adapted from* Mrs. Lincoln's Boston Cook Book *(1884), compiled by Boston Cooking School teacher Mary Lincoln. This gives the salad extra zing and an added layer of depth.*

SERVES 4

¼ teaspoon salt

⅛ teaspoon pepper

3 tablespoons olive oil

1 tablespoon tarragon or white wine vinegar

2½ cups cooked lobster meat

2 stalks celery

1 small head iceberg or Boston lettuce

3–4 tablespoons mayonnaise, homemade (see page 113) or store bought

Capers, parsley, and lobster claws, for garnish

Make a marinade by whisking salt, pepper, olive oil, and vinegar in a medium bowl until well mixed.

Cut lobster in 1-inch dice and celery in ½-inch dice. Add to the bowl with the marinade. Chill in the fridge for at least 2 hours.

While lobster is marinating, wash and separate lettuce leaves. Set leaves on a clean kitchen towel to dry.

Remove lobster from the fridge and add mayonnaise to taste. To plate, place lettuce leaves on a platter, making a cup shape with the rounded side down, trimming any excess around the edges if necessary. Place a large spoonful of the salad in each leaf, topping each with a dollop of mayonnaise if desired. Garnish with capers, sprigs of parsley, and lobster claws.

Queenie's Cornmeal Potato Muffins

While New York society was famous for having summer homes in Newport, Rhode Island, others chose to escape the winter cold in the Northeast for warmer locations. Mina and Thomas Edison headed to their estate in Fort Myers, Florida, which they called Seminole Lodge, built in 1886. Their good friend Henry Ford later joined them and bought a house next door. The Edisons brought their African American cook Queenie Adams with them to Florida, where one newspaper hailed her as much a wizard in the kitchen as Edison was in his laboratory. This recipe is adapted from the Edison's Family and Friends Recipes *booklet published by the Edison and Ford Winter Estates in Fort Myers.*

MAKES 1 DOZEN

1 cup cooked mashed potatoes, warm
1 egg, beaten
1 cup milk
2 tablespoons vegetable oil
1 cup yellow cornmeal
4 teaspoons baking powder
2 tablespoons sugar
1 teaspoon salt
1 cup shredded cheddar cheese

Preheat oven to 350°F. Grease a 12-cup muffin tin with butter or cooking spray and set aside.

Place the mashed potatoes in a large bowl, then add the egg, milk, and vegetable oil stirring to mix well.

In a smaller bowl, combine the cornmeal, baking powder, sugar, and salt. Add to the potato mixture and stir until just mixed. Fold in the shredded cheddar cheese.

Scoop the batter into the muffin cups and bake for 15 minutes.

Contributed by food historian and culinary stylist Dan Macey

Sponge Cake

Simple, light, and elegant, sponge cake was the quintessential cake of the Gilded Age, transformed into endless style and flavor combinations. Some were served plain, garnished simply with a sprinkling of confectioners' sugar. Others took it up a notch by adding flavorings such as orange or lemon, such as this version adapted from the manuscript cookbook of Lydia Morris, compiled over three decades starting in 1883. Lydia and her brother John purchased twenty-six acres of farmland in the Chestnut Hill section of Philadelphia in 1887, where they built Compton, an estate with a large mansion and extensive gardens. Now known as the Morris Arboretum, it is the site of many educational and research programs.

SERVES 12–16

2½ cups granulated sugar
1 lemon
10 eggs, separated
Pinch of salt
3⅓ cups all-purpose flour, sifted
Confectioners' sugar (optional)
Fresh strawberries and whipped cream (optional)

Bring all ingredients to room temperature. Remove top rack of oven and preheat to 325°F.

Place sugar in a small bowl. Using a microplane or fine zester, grate lemon peel into the sugar. Extract juice from the lemon and strain through a fine sieve.

Using an electric mixer, beat egg yolks in a large bowl on medium speed until just mixed (about 1 minute). Add sugar and lemon juice and beat on high for about 4–5 minutes or until mixture is thick and light yellow in color.

In a separate glass or stainless steel bowl, beat egg whites and pinch of salt on low speed until foamy, about 3–4 minutes, then increase speed to medium and continue to beat another 5–8 minutes or until stiff. Fold into yolk mixture, then add flour a little at a time, folding in gently (do not overmix).

Pour batter into an ungreased 10-inch tube pan and smooth the top. Bake for 1 hour.

Remove from oven and stand cake upside down on the neck of a bottle until completely cooled, about 1½–2 hours. To remove the cake from the pan, take a long, sharp knife or metal spatula and run it around the inside of the pan to loosen the cake from the sides, then gently remove the pan's center core. Next, run the knife or spatula along the bottom and center core to loosen. Carefully remove the bottom of the pan and invert the cake on a serving plate.

To serve, sprinkle with confectioners' sugar and cut into slices. Pass with fresh sliced strawberries and whipped cream (see recipe on page 83) if desired.

Wedding Breakfast, New York, New York, circa 1900–1910 HISTORY SAN JOSE PHOTOGRAPHIC COLLECTION

WEDDING BREAKFASTS

Gilded Age brides often opted to have a midday wedding followed by a wedding breakfast. Depending on the number of people invited, these events could range from simple to extravagant, held in either the bride's home or an off-site location. Flowers were an important part of the décor. White was the preferred color, with roses, carnations, narcissus, and violets the most common, tied with white ribbon and accented by feathery ferns. A single white rosebud or floral spray was placed by each place setting, alongside bread sticks wrapped in a napkin and tied together with narrow white ribbon. Small dishes of relishes, crisp celery, olives, salted nuts, and bonbons encircled the large floral centerpiece. Place cards, china, and serving dishes were cream or muted colors with accents of pale yellow, violet, or green. Candelabras with little white shades made from silk or delicate tissue paper were placed at each end of the table. The wedding cake, elaborately embellished with white icing, was situated directly in front of the bride, who would have the honor of cutting it at the end of the meal.

If a formal affair (over fifty guests), the guests would be seated at small tables for six, with special distinction given to the wedding table. The multi-course meal was kicked off with a frozen drink such as puree of Malaga grapes

John Trower

Many Gilded Age wedding breakfasts in and around Philadelphia were catered by John Trower, an extremely successful caterer, businessman, and philanthropist who was considered among the wealthiest African Americans in Pennsylvania at the time. Born in Virginia in 1849 to farmers Luke and Anna Trower, he headed to Baltimore in 1870 with just $52 in his pocket and worked his way up in the restaurant industry, eventually heading to Philadelphia. He saved enough to start a catering business in the city's Germantown section, where he catered to the elite from all over the Northeast, including department store merchant John Wanamaker and US presidents Benjamin Harrison and Grover Cleveland.

Trower's elegant wedding breakfasts were legendary throughout the area. One such event in 1890 took place in the private home of the bride's parents in Pottsville, Pennsylvania. Items were set on a large exquisitely appointed table in the dining room, centered around Blue Point oysters set on graceful swans cut from clear ice and pyramids of cake and cream. Other items on the menu included chicken salad, oyster croquettes, chicken croquettes, lobster salad, lobster cutlets, terrapin, salmon, boned turkey, rasped rolls, meringues, ice creams and water ices, charlotte russe, assorted fruits, cake, and coffee. Another wedding he catered in 1906 had two separate menus: one for the guests (served in the dining room), which included deviled crabs, chicken croquettes and peas, sweetbread patties, chicken salad, rasped rolls, ice cream and ices, strawberries, cake, bonbons, lemonade, and coffee, and another for the bridal party (served upstairs), which featured strawberries in baskets, cream of chicken, spring chicken, watercress, new peas and potatoes, Roman punch, asparagus salad with French dressing, rolls, cheese and crackers, fancy creams, jellies, cake, bonbons, and coffee.

Roosevelt Wedding Breakfast in the White House

On February 17, 1906, President Theodore Roosevelt's daughter Alice married Nicholas Longworth, a congressman from Ohio, in the East Room at the White House. It was the most talked-about social event of Roosevelt's presidency and made the front page of newspapers throughout the country. The guest list was reportedly in the one thousand range and is still considered the largest White House wedding ever. Those attending the ceremony included members of the "Four Hundred," including Caroline Astor, Mr. and Mrs. Robert Goelet, and Mr. and Mrs. Cornelius Vanderbilt.

After the ceremony, guests were received by President and Mrs. Roosevelt in the Blue Parlor before proceeding into the walnut-paneled state dining room for the wedding breakfast. There all the food was laid out in buffet form on a forty-foot table. Flower arrangements were of deep pink American Beauty and soft pink bride roses, accented by delicate ferns and asparagus flowers. Similar to the standing luncheons popular at the time (see page 160), there were no seats, but plenty of waiters were on hand to serve the guests. Smaller tables held large punch bowls and glasses for wine and mineral water. The menu included salads, cold meats, croquettes, ices, coffee, and cake. The bridal party and close friends had their meal in the adjoining family dining room. The doors remained open so guests could mill in and out, extending well wishes and witnessing the cutting of the wedding cake. Said to have been two and a half feet in diameter, the cake was so immense that it required three waiters to bring it out to the table and a sword to cut it, which young Alice borrowed from Marine officer Charles McCawley.

Floral arrangements, Alice Roosevelt's wedding, 1906 FLICKR COMMONS

or iced pomegranate in punch glasses, followed by a soup course of clam bouillon served with bread sticks, then a fish course of fillet of sole, sauce tartare, accompanied by soufflé potatoes. Sweetbread patties would be next, then a main course of pigeon cutlets or chicken croquettes with green peas or potatoes, followed by a salad course of Waldorf salad, celery mayonnaise, or tomato jelly, accompanied by wafers or cheese straws. Then came the dessert course featuring charlotte russe, ices molded into decorative shapes, and fancy cakes, ending with coffee served in small after-dinner cups along with bonbons and other confections. Small crystal finger-bowls half filled with lukewarm water and topped with a tiny rosebud would be brought out after the dessert to allow guests to rinse off their fingers.

If the wedding was smaller in size, guests were often seated at one long table like a dinner party. The menu was also typically less formal, including dishes such as baked bananas, broiled shad with roe sauce, Parisienne potatoes, breaded lamb chops with tomato sauce, French rolls, sweetbread cutlets with cream sauce, French peas, melon, and charlotte russe.

Chicken Croquettes

Croquettes are little nuggets of ground meat or vegetables bound with eggs or a sauce, coated in bread crumbs and then fried until golden and crunchy on the outside. The name comes from their deliciously crispy exterior; "croquette" is derived from the French verb croquer, *or "crunch." These flavorful delicacies were very popular during the Gilded Age, found throughout cookbooks from the era and at large catered events such as weddings and receptions. The most important thing about this recipe is to mince the chicken very fine (I use my food processor).*

SERVES 8

2 cups cold cooked chicken
1 teaspoon salt
1 teaspoon pepper
⅛ teaspoon cayenne pepper
¼ teaspoon mace
½ tablespoon lemon juice
1 tablespoon minced onion
½ tablespoon finely chopped parsley
3 tablespoons unsalted butter
5 tablespoons all-purpose flour
1 cup milk or stock
1 large egg
2 cups fine bread crumbs
Canola or vegetable oil

Finely chop the chicken or place in the bowl of a food processor and pulse until minced. Add the salt, pepper, cayenne, mace, lemon juice, onion, and parsley and mix until combined.

Melt the butter in a large saucepan over medium heat. Whisk in the flour until smooth, then gradually whisk in the milk or stock. Bring to a boil and cook until thickened, about 2 minutes, stirring constantly.

Add the chicken to the sauce and mix well. Remove from heat and transfer the chicken mixture to a large bowl or platter. Cover and place in the refrigerator for about 1 hour to chill.

Break the egg into a small bowl and whisk for about 30 seconds. Place the bread crumbs in a separate shallow dish.

Chicken Croquettes

Remove the chicken mixture from the refrigerator. With wet hands, form into small round or cone shapes. Roll each lightly in bread crumbs, dip in the egg, and then fully coat with bread crumbs and place on a clean platter.

When done forming the croquette shapes, heat ½ inch of oil over medium-high heat in a deep cast-iron skillet. When shimmering, fry 3–4 croquettes at a time, turning twice, until golden brown, about 3 minutes (don't fry too many at a time or the boiling oil will cool too much and the croquettes will become greasy). Transfer to a wire rack or paper towels set on a baking sheet to cool and drain. Repeat with the remaining chicken mixture. Serve immediately.

Asparagus Salad with French Dressing

Asparagus was a beloved Gilded Age vegetable, often served in salad form at weddings. It was so popular, the 1909 book One Thousand Salads *by Olive Green lists a dozen asparagus salad recipes, all with different garnishes and dressings. The following recipe was featured in an 1897 issue of* American Kitchen Magazine.

SERVES 4–6

FOR THE SALAD:

1 bunch fresh asparagus

Green or red leaf lettuce, washed and dried, leaves separated

¼ teaspoon salt

¼ teaspoon white pepper

FOR THE FRENCH DRESSING:

¼ teaspoon salt

¼ teaspoon white pepper

½ teaspoon onion powder

3 tablespoons olive oil, divided

1 tablespoon white wine vinegar

½ tablespoon lemon juice

Place asparagus in a colander and rinse with cold water. Break off the tough bottom ends and discard.

Transfer asparagus to a large skillet and cover with water and a pinch of salt. Bring to a boil over high heat and then turn down to low and simmer for 3–5 minutes or desired tenderness.

Drain asparagus in the colander and rinse with cold water. Let it drain while you make the dressing.

To make the dressing, combine salt, white pepper, onion powder, and 1 tablespoon olive oil in a small bowl. Stir with a whisk, then alternately add the rest of the oil, vinegar, and lemon juice, whisking well. Set aside.

Pat the asparagus dry with a towel and then cut into 1-inch diagonal pieces. To plate the salad, place the lettuce in an oblong dish or bowl and arrange the asparagus on top. Sprinkle with salt and white pepper. Pour dressing over the top to taste, reserving extra for the table. Serve immediately.

Lady Cake

Lady cake is a rich pound cake flavored with almonds and rosewater, made snowy white by using only egg whites. Its white color and delicate texture were considered so exquisite and elegant that it was often used as a wedding cake in the Gilded Age, frosted with pure white icing and decorated with white flowers. According to nineteenth-century cookbook writer Eliza Leslie, "This cake is beautifully white, and (if the recipe is strictly followed) will be found delicious. If well made, and quite fresh, there is no cake better liked." Her recipe was apparently for a large wedding-type cake since she stipulates using "the whites only of sixteen eggs, three quarters of a pound of sifted flour, half a pound of fresh butter and a pound of powdered white sugar."

SERVES 12–16

6 egg whites
2 sticks (1 cup) unsalted butter, softened
1¾ cups sugar
2¾ cups cake flour
2 teaspoons baking powder
1¼ cups milk
1 tablespoon rosewater
2 teaspoons almond extract

Butter a 10-inch Bundt pan, dust the inside with flour, and set aside. Adjust the oven rack to the lower position and preheat to 350°F.

Place the egg whites in a large glass or stainless steel bowl. Using an electric mixer, beat on low speed until soft peaks form, about 3–4 minutes, then increase speed to medium and continue to beat until stiff, about another 5–8 minutes. Set aside.

In a separate bowl, cream the butter on medium-high until very fluffy. Slowly add the sugar, about ¼ cup at a time, until the mixture is a creamy texture.

Sift the flour and baking powder together. Alternately add the dry ingredients and the milk to the butter mixture, mixing between additions.

Add the rosewater and almond extract. Stir and scrape the batter down. Gently fold in the egg whites (best done by hand).

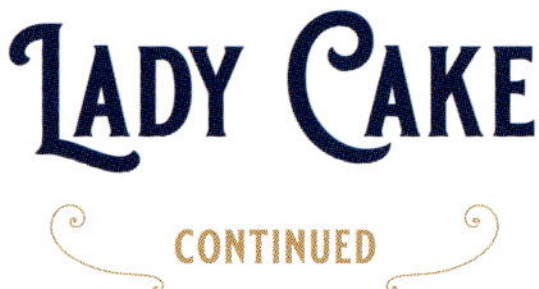

Spoon the cake batter into the Bundt pan and smooth the top. Bake for 50–60 minutes or until a toothpick inserted into the center comes out clean. Cool on a wire rack for 20 minutes and then run a sharp knife around the edge to loosen. Invert on a plate to cool completely.

Sprinkle with confectioners' sugar and serve with fresh fruit and/or whipped cream, or frost with egg white icing.

EGG WHITE ICING

2 egg whites, room temperature

2 cups confectioners' sugar

1 teaspoon rosewater

Using an electric mixer, whip the egg whites on low speed until they form soft peaks, about 3–4 minutes. Increase the speed to medium and gradually add the sugar 1 cup at a time. Add rosewater and beat on medium-high speed for another 5–8 minutes or until the icing forms medium to stiff peaks.

NOTE: *This icing should be used within one day. For those leery of using egg whites, you can substitute ¼ cup meringue powder and ½ cup cold water for the fresh egg whites.*

Shrewsbury Cakes

These delightful little cakes are crispy on the outside and slightly soft on the inside. A fragrant combination of cinnamon and rosewater gives them a delicate, slightly spicy flavor. They are often embellished with a pretty design, made by scoring the dough with a knife and then glazing with beaten egg. The name comes from their place of origin—the British medieval market town of Shrewsbury. They later made their way over to America, where they became a teatime staple. Little cakes of this type would have been served alongside ices and ice creams at Gilded Age wedding breakfasts, sometimes as a special treat for the bridesmaids.

FOR THE CAKES:

6 tablespoons salted butter, softened

⅓ cup sugar

2 large eggs

1 teaspoon rosewater or orange flower water

2 cups all-purpose flour

½ teaspoon cinnamon

FOR THE GLAZE:

1 large egg

1 teaspoon sugar

Preheat oven to 350°F.

Cream butter and sugar in a medium bowl with an electric mixer until smooth, scraping bowl down if necessary. Add eggs one at a time and mix well, then add rosewater.

Sift flour with cinnamon and then slowly add to the other ingredients. Mix until a soft dough forms.

Form dough into a ball and roll out onto a well-floured surface to a ¼-inch thickness. Cut into shapes using a biscuit or cookie cutter. Transfer to cookie sheets lined with parchment paper. Using a knife, draw flowers, leaves, or any other design of your choice on each.

Make a glaze by beating an egg and 1 teaspoon sugar in a small bowl. Use a pastry brush to generously glaze the cakes with the beaten egg and sugar mixture.

Bake for 10–12 minutes or until firm to the touch. Sprinkle with granulated or colored sugar if desired. Cool on a wire rack.

Tea Party Table, Mrs. Beeton's Book of Household Management, *1907 edition* WIKIMEDIA COMMONS

TEA PARTIES

We can thank England's Anna Russell for first making "afternoon tea" into a formal social occasion. Also known as the Duchess of Bedford, Anna was one of Queen Victoria's ladies-in-waiting. The origins had to do with the shifting hour of the evening meal, which became fashionably later (around 8:00 to 9:00 p.m.) as advancements in lighting—first gas, then electricity—enabled houses to stay lit until well into the late evening. As a result, Anna understandably began to feel hungry in the late afternoon and requested a spot of tea and some light food, which probably included bread, butter, and perhaps biscuits.

The idea proved so successful that it soon became routine, and the duchess decided to invite a few of her friends to her private rooms for tea in the afternoon, spawning a new social opportunity for the upper classes. Americans soon caught on to the idea, adding afternoon tea (sometimes referred to as "five o'clock tea") to their Gilded Age entertaining methods. Invitations would be sent out ten days before the date of the tea to all the people on the hostess's visiting list, including husbands, wives, grandparents, grown children, and cousins. It was a way to meet with friends and acquaintances and form new ones,

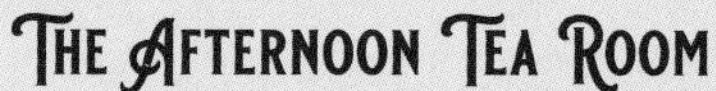

The Afternoon Tea Room

In 1896, two enterprising women, Ellin Prince Lowery and Margaret Wilmerding, launched the Afternoon Tea Room on Fifth Avenue in New York. Lowery was orphaned as a child and raised by her uncle, lawyer William Travers, and Wilmerding was the sister of merchant Frederick Wilmerding. Both were prominent and active members of New York society, playing host to numerous charitable events. They had the idea to open a tearoom in New York after seeing similar successful ventures in Paris. The intention was to provide both a place for women to have lunch as they were out shopping and a convenient location for New York society to drop in for a cup of afternoon tea. Moderately priced, it was open to all—a membership fee was not required like societal clubs. Although the tearoom catered to women, men were welcome too. It was a progressive move, particularly since it was still often considered improper for women to dine at eating establishments unaccompanied by men.

The tearoom's feminine décor included pale rose satin wallpaper with a silver-edged plate glass mirror border. Pink and violet drapes framed the windows, and silver stars sparkled against the backdrop of a pure-white ceiling. Small tables were located around the room, covered by white damask tablecloths edged with Irish lace and topped with fresh bouquets of violets. Open from noon to 6:00 p.m., the tearoom served a light luncheon as well as afternoon tea, featuring items such as drop cakes, buns, gingerbread, sponge cake, and waffles served on elegant china, cut-glass dishes, and heirloom family silver.

Soon similar tearooms began cropping up all over New York's shopping district, including inside department stores such as Wanamaker's and hotels like the Waldorf, which turned its Palm Room (formerly a men's bar) into a tearoom. And other women soon picked up on the idea to try their hand as business operators, with over one hundred of these tearooms owned and managed by women by the early 1900s, estimated the *Sun*. But some papers actually criticized the trend, claiming the "custom is doing away with all social life in the late afternoon . . . It is useless to try to do much entertaining on one's own account, since people prefer to meet one another downtown."

arrange plans for future get-togethers, and pay off social obligations—all without much expense or late hours.

Like a receiving line at a wedding, the hostess would stand by the drawing-room door and greet each guest in turn. After exchanging a few brief words, guests would enter the dining room, where a large table spread with a crisp white linen cloth was decorated with artfully arranged cut flowers, including a large centerpiece in the middle and four corner-pieces. It was fashionable to pick a specific color scheme for the flowers, such as pink, white, or red roses or yellow daffodils and jonquils.

Tea Party Sweets, Mrs. Beeton's Book of Household Management, *1923 edition* WIKIMEDIA COMMONS

One end of the table was reserved for the tea service, featuring a teapot and cozy, sugar bowl, creamer, and tongs, along with cups, saucers, spoons, piles of plates and napkins, and plates of sliced lemon and fancy cakes. The hot chocolate service was at the other end, including a chocolate pot, cups, saucers, spoons, plates, napkins, sugar cubes and tongs, whipped cream and spoon, and cakes. If iced drinks were offered, they would also be placed at opposite ends; for example, a bowl of frappé at one end and frozen cherries on the other. Small glass cups and teaspoons would be laid out conveniently nearby, with dishes containing fancy cakes placed strategically on each corner of the table. Coffee would be on the sideboard, including a coffee urn filled with strong black coffee, with small coffee cups, saucers, and spoons nearby.

More napkins, sugar cubes, whipped cream, cakes, and serving plates would round out the coffee service.

The food at tea parties was actually fairly simple—fancy cakes and small tea sandwiches were the only requisite foods. Some hostesses liked to add other items to the serving list, including strawberries or other fruit, bouillon, rolled sandwiches, bonbons, and salted nuts. In addition, frozen cherries, caffi frappé (frozen coffee), and/or biscuits glacé (little squares of ice cream served in individual paper cases) became trendy during the Gilded Age. But none of these items were "required" as per social etiquette of the time.

Of course, having these enormous amounts of dishes at a tea was dependent on having someone in the kitchen for the express purpose of washing dishes. One or two servants were also recommended to carry away soiled cups and saucers and keep the table looking clean and fresh. But the duty of pouring the tea and chocolate was given to a "lady"—typically a pretty girl or charming married woman. Like the hostess, she would wear a gown closed to the throat, since full dress before dinner was considered extremely improper. In addition, even though guests wore bonnets, the ladies of the house did not.

A five o'clock tea could also be more intimate and informal. According to an 1892 *Good Housekeeping* article, these teas would feature a dainty embroidered tea cloth laid out on a small table—round if possible—with two or three choice cups and saucers, teaspoons, a small sugar bowl with sugar tongs, a small cream jug, a dish of bonbons, and a small teapot of freshly made tea. Hot bouillon and rolled bread and butter sandwiches were sometimes offered as well. A young lady of the family would be on duty to sit and make tea, which was considered more sociable, and gentlemen were given the job of serving it to everyone.

Dainty Tea Sandwiches

Tea sandwiches were a savory supplement to the sweet cakes and cookies served at Gilded Age afternoon tea parties. This was particularly the case if gentlemen guests were present, "whose appetites require something more substantial than tea and cake," according to an 1895 American Kitchen Magazine *article by pure foods lecturer Eliza R. Parker. Fillings included meats such as mutton, veal, and potted rabbit; fish such as salmon, anchovy, or sardines; and dairy-based spreads such as eggs and cheese. Parker's original recipe for cheese sandwiches calls for Roquefort, but I have substituted Gorgonzola since Roquefort is banned in the United States due to the presence of* E. coli *bacteria.*

CHEESE SANDWICHES

1 (5-ounce) package crumbled Gorgonzola cheese, softened

2 tablespoons unsalted butter, softened

1 tablespoon minced parsley

12 slices thin sliced bread (like Pepperidge Farm Very Thin Sliced Bread)

Place the cheese in a medium bowl and mash it with the back of a fork or a pastry cutter until it is a soft, creamy consistency. Add butter and parsley and stir until well mixed.

Spread 2 tablespoons of the cheese mixture on half of the bread slices, then top with remaining slices. Trim crusts from the sandwiches, then cut each into 3 oblong (finger length) pieces. Chill in the refrigerator until ready to serve.

Dainty Tea Sandwiches

CONTINUED

CURRY SANDWICHES

MAKES 12 TRIANGLE SANDWICHES

6 hard-boiled egg yolks

2 tablespoons unsalted butter, softened

2 teaspoons Worcestershire sauce

1 tablespoon curry powder

¼ teaspoon salt

2 tablespoons bread crumbs

2 teaspoons white wine vinegar

Butter, softened (for spreading)

12 slices thin sliced bread (like Pepperidge Farm Very Thin Sliced Bread)

Place egg yolks, butter, Worcestershire sauce, curry powder, salt, and bread crumbs in a medium bowl and mash with the back of a fork until smooth. Add vinegar a little at a time until mixture is a spreadable consistency.

Spread half the bread slices with butter, then 1½ tablespoons of the curry mixture. Top with remaining bread slices. Trim crusts from sandwiches, then cut each sandwich into triangles. Chill in the refrigerator until ready to serve. Garnish with nasturtiums or other edible flowers if desired.

Tea Cakes

Similar to shortbread, these buttery, tasty little cakes are perfect for tea as their name suggests. Most cookbooks from the nineteenth century feature at least one recipe for tea cakes, which was often a category in itself. There were several variations—some called for a flavoring such as nutmeg, cinnamon, or rosewater and others used yeast and/or milk to make the dough rise, resulting in a lighter confection, more like a true cake or light biscuit.

MAKES 2½ DOZEN

2½ cups all-purpose flour
⅛ teaspoon salt
¼ cup sugar
2 large eggs, beaten
1 stick (½ cup) unsalted butter, melted
Cold water
1 egg yolk, beaten
Additional granulated sugar

Preheat oven to 375°F.

Sift the flour with the salt into a large bowl. Add the sugar, eggs, and melted butter and stir together, adding cold water a teaspoon at a time to make a rather stiff paste.

Transfer the dough to a pasteboard or clean counter dusted with flour. Knead into a ball and then roll to about ¼-inch thickness. Cut the dough into shapes with a cookie cutter, or roll into a log shape and slice into ¼-inch-thick circles. Place on baking sheets lined with parchment paper.

Brush the top of each cake with beaten egg yolk and then sprinkle with sugar. Bake for 10–12 minutes. Cool on wire racks.

Jumbles

Originally shaped like a figure eight or double ring, the name jumble comes from the Latin word gemel, *which means "twin." Since this was a time-consuming shape for a cookie, it became customary for Americans to form the dough into single rings. By the Gilded Age, many cooks rolled out the dough, cut it into rounds, and then stamped out the middles (like doughnuts). The dough was often flavored with freshly grated nutmeg and sometimes also cinnamon and/or mace, as well as rosewater or lemon essence, resulting in a unique taste combination that is both spicy and delicate.*

2 sticks (1 cup) unsalted butter, softened
1 cup sugar
1 large egg
1 tablespoon rosewater (or lemon essence)
3 cups all-purpose flour
2 teaspoons ground nutmeg
½ teaspoon mace
½ teaspoon cinnamon
Additional granulated sugar

Preheat oven to 375°F.

Cream butter and sugar in a large bowl with an electric mixer until very light. Add egg and rosewater, blending thoroughly.

Sift the flour with nutmeg, mace, and cinnamon. Add to the butter mixture, mixing to form a soft dough. Wrap dough and chill in the refrigerator for at least 2 hours.

Lightly flour a pasteboard or counter and roll out the dough to ¼-inch thickness. Cut into strips 1 by 8 inches and shape into rings. Or, cut into circles using a round cookie cutter or glass turned upside down and stamp out the middles with a thimble to make ring shapes. Place on baking sheets with parchment paper.

Bake for 10–12 minutes or until lightly browned around edges, rotating once. Remove to a wire rack and sprinkle with sugar.

Opposite: Ebenezer Maxwell Mansion, Philadelphia, Pennsylvania

Chocolate Puffs

Deliciously chewy with a slightly crispy coating, chocolate puffs are delightful meringue cookies reminiscent of a baked chocolate mousse. According to the original recipe from the 1884 cookbook Culinary Gems: A Collection of Choice Recipes Gathered with Care from the Treasures of Culinary Experts, *chocolate puffs are "nice to mix with cake in the basket," so they were likely served for tea, perhaps in a silver basket covered with lace, arranged alongside golden sponge cake and dark, rich fruitcake. The contrasting shades of these treats would have been a lovely presentation.*

MAKES ABOUT 2½ DOZEN

2 ounces (½ package) unsweetened baking chocolate
2 tablespoons cornstarch
2 egg whites
Pinch of cream of tartar
1 cup confectioners' sugar

Preheat oven to 350°F.

Grate the chocolate into a medium bowl using a microplate or other fine grater. Add cornstarch and stir until blended. Set aside.

Using an electric mixer, beat the egg whites in a stainless steel or glass bowl at a low to medium speed. Add the cream of tartar after 2 minutes, or when the egg white foam increases in volume with smaller bubbles.

Increase the mixer speed to medium. When the bubbles become smaller and more even in size, increase the mixer speed to medium-high. Add the sugar slowly in a steady stream at the side of the bowl.

Increase the mixer speed to high and continue beating until the meringue is white, fluffy, firm, and still very glossy, like white cake icing. Add the chocolate mixture slowly until fully incorporated.

Drop spoonfuls of meringue on parchment paper–lined baking sheets and bake for 15 minutes. Cool on baking sheets for about 30 minutes and then transfer to a wire rack to cool completely.

CHAPTER FIVE

HOLIDAYS

THANKSGIVING

Roast Turkey with Dressing and Chicken Forcemeat Balls

Sweet Potato Croquettes

Crisp Celery

Pumpkin Cake

Baked Apple Pudding

CHRISTMAS

Steamed Halibut with Egg Sauce

Peas Served in Turnip Cups

Deviled Spaghetti

Lemon Star Cookies

Gâteaux de Milan

Plum Pudding

Sugar Plums

TWELFTH NIGHT

Twelfth Night Cake

The strain of preparing a dinner falls directly upon the woman of the household, and it matters not whether she has to cook it herself or has servants do it for her. . . . As every woman knows—if every man doesn't—a good dinner, be it on Christmas or any other day, requires personal supervision, [even] though it [may] be cooked by other hands.

—*LADIES HOME JOURNAL*, DECEMBER 1894

EXTENSIVE MENUS featuring rich, appealing foods were a key part of Gilded Age holiday celebrations. This chapter highlights popular recipes from the era. Although many are still favorites today, such as roast turkey with stuffing, cranberry jelly, and mashed potatoes, others are not often seen on modern dinner tables, including sweet potato croquettes, peas served in turnip cups, and deviled spaghetti.

THANKSGIVING

Gilded Age Thanksgiving celebrations were sophisticated events with an emphasis on décor and elegance. Harvest-themed decorations such as autumn leaves, chrysanthemums, asters, dried grasses, and grains would be placed throughout the house, particularly the dining room. Fresh fruit piled high on a silver or pewter platter, embellished with vines and clusters of grapes, would create a stunning centerpiece. Other dining table decorations included fruit-filled cornucopias and baskets of chrysanthemums and other autumn flowers. If the dinner

Gilded Age Thanksgiving, Ebenezer Maxwell Mansion, Philadelphia

Godey's Lady's Book

Godey's Lady's Book was an influential magazine published in Philadelphia aimed toward educating and entertaining an ever-expanding audience of American women. Launched in 1830, Sarah Josepha Hale was the popular publication's editor for forty years, from 1837 to 1877. Hale was not only a prominent advocate of making Thanksgiving a national holiday, but also helped promulgate and merge a variety of practices into modern holiday traditions through the magazine's suggestions and advice columns for holiday entertaining. For example, while we think of today's Thanksgiving celebration as a gluttonous, food-filled feast, it was an even larger meal in the late 1800s. "His Birdship [the turkey] is brought on after the soup and fish course, and is removed in depleted glory to make room for the a la mode beef that comes next at Thanksgiving feasts to-day," noted writer Augusta Salisbury Prescott in the magazine's November 1890 issue as part of a year-long series discussing American traditions called "A Year in the Home."

Thanksgiving Becomes a National Holiday

Thanksgiving celebrations in America originated out of the desire to give thanks for a specific event, such as a bountiful harvest or beneficial rainfall. These days were randomly declared by ministers or governors within a specific region and were religious in focus, although they came to involve sharing an abundance of food with family and friends. On October 3, 1789, President George Washington issued a proclamation designating November 26 of that year as a National Day of Thanksgiving for US citizens, to give thanks for their newly created nation and federal Constitution. Public festivities were held, and Washington himself celebrated the day by attending services at St. Paul's Chapel in New York City and doing a bit of philanthropy (donating beer and food to imprisoned debtors in the city). But Washington's proclamation did not establish an annual "Thanksgiving Day," although he did issue another proclamation in February 1795 to recognize the defeat of a tax rebellion in Pennsylvania.

Later on, other presidents announced one-time Days of Thanksgiving, with no specific date attached. By the 1850s, almost every state and territory celebrated Thanksgiving, but it wasn't until President Abraham Lincoln issued a proclamation in 1863 that it became a national holiday, the result of a seventeen-year campaign by *Godey's Lady's Book* editor Sarah Josepha Hale. She was able to convince Lincoln that a national Thanksgiving might help heal the nation after the devastating Civil War. At this time it was given the standard date of the last Thursday in November, although in 1941 Congress passed a law making Thanksgiving the fourth Thursday of November to allow retailers to rein in more shoppers between Thanksgiving and Christmas.

was served in the late afternoon, the hostess would often close the blinds, illuminating the room with soft, mellow candlelight. A glowing fireplace provided an atmosphere of comfort and good cheer. As an 1899 issue of *Table Talk* magazine advised "an air of festivity should pervade the home."

The meal preparations were similar to the way we plan our Thanksgiving meal today, with much of the cooking done in advance. Items like puddings

Lakewood Resorts and Thanksgiving

Located in Ocean County, New Jersey, the township of Lakewood was a popular fall and winter resort during the Gilded Age. When the New Jersey Southern Railroad arrived in 1863, development in the area took off, and several splendid hotels were built throughout the following decades. Convenient rail service from both New York and Philadelphia allowed upper-class society from both areas to escape to the huge resorts, which were promoted as having a milder climate and fresh, pine-scented air that could supposedly cure pulmonary ailments. Two of the most famous hotels opened in 1891: Laurel-in-the-Pines and the Lakewood Hotel.

The Lakewood

Lakewood, N.J.

DINNER

Blue Point Oysters — Special Parisien Bread

Russian Caviar — Celery — Olives — Sliced Tomatoes

SOUPS

Consommé Charmel — Cream of Sweet Corn, Croutons Soufflé

Broth Plain — Cocki-lecki á l'Ecossaise

FISH

Red Snapper, Portugaise Sauce — Filet of Flondres, Normande

Bermuda Potatoes

JOINTS

Loin of Beef with Cabbage, Braisé — Leg of Mutton Boiled, Caper Sauce

ENTREES

Squab Compote with Mushrooms

Tenderloin of Beef, Lardé, Espagnola Sauce

Escalope of Veal, Pané, Jardiniere

Macaroni, Calabraise

ROAST

Turkey, Cranberry Sauce

Lamb, Mint Sauce

Ribs of Beef

Game Pie with Jelly

VEGETABLES

Cauliflower, Hollandaise Sauce — Green Peppers Stuffed — Mashed Potatoes

Rice Boiled — Stewed Tomatoes — Onions, Cream Sauce

Sweet Potatoes Boiled

SALADS

Chicory — Hot House Lettuce — Celery

ENTREMET CHAUD

Apples á la Francaise

PASTRY

Apricot Pie — Rhubarb Pie — Charlotte Russe

Chocolate Eclaires — Genoise Roulé — Jelly Kirsh

Petits Choux Grilié — Macaroons — Petits Fours Assortie

ICE CREAM

Sorbet Calvados — Vanille — Strawberry — Pistache — Lemon

DESSERT

Bananas — Florida Oranges — Grapes — Almonds — Apples — Pecan Nuts

English Walnuts — Raisins

CHEESE

American — Stilton — Edam — Cream

Holland Gouda — Roquefort — Imported Brie — Imported Camenbert

Graham Crackers — Bents Crackers

Saturday, April 1, 1893. — SEE OTHER SIDE. —

Dinner menu, The Lakewood [Hotel], Lakewood, New Jersey, 1893

Thanksgiving marked the opening of Lakewood's social season, which included activities such as the Lakewood Golf Club Thanksgiving tournament, horse racing, carriage rides around Lake Drive, evening symphony concerts, and a Thanksgiving bazaar given by the Ladies' Aid Society of All Saints' Church. Gilded Age society who frequented Lakewood included the Vanderbilts, Astors, Rockefellers, Tilfords, and Goulds, as well as President Grover Cleveland, Tammany Hall political boss Richard Croker, writers Rudyard Kipling and Oliver Wendell Holmes, and publishers Joseph Pulitzer and Charles Scribner. Many of these people built stunning homes in the area, including the John D. Rockefeller Estate (now Ocean County Park), the Grover Cleveland Cottage, and Georgian Court, an estate built by George Jay Gould and now home to Georgian Court University.

Thanksgiving Card, 1908 NEW YORK PUBLIC LIBRARY

and mincemeat were made at least a week or two ahead, which also allowed the flavors to blend. Women's magazines from the time also recommended never trying a new recipe without first testing it in smaller proportions. The goal was striking a balance between old and new traditions.

Before the mid-nineteenth century, it was customary to bring out all the Thanksgiving food at once. But the Gilded Age ushered in the *à la russe* style of dining, where dinner was served in multiple courses. As a result, the meal would typically start with oyster soup or bouillon, then a second course featuring roast turkey, stuffing, and cranberry jelly, followed by a cleansing sorbet to restore the palate. The next course was chicken pie, accompanied by stewed corn, mashed potatoes, and squash, followed by a salad course of celery, wafers, and cheese. Desserts were often served in two parts—a first course of Thanksgiving pudding, pumpkin pie, cake, and ice cream, and a final course of fruit, bonbons, and nuts. Coffee was offered at the very end of the meal, sometimes at the table, but most hostesses preferred to serve it in the parlor.

Thanksgiving was one occasion where children, parents, grandparents, aunts, uncles, and cousins all came together. The needs of children were actually considered, including special arrangements such as a large hall or

Autumn in Newport

A large number of Gilded Age "cottagers" lengthened their summer season by remaining in Newport long after Labor Day, often lingering until Thanksgiving. To fill their time, they held dinner parties, luncheons, and sailing and fishing trips. Many hosted large Thanksgiving gatherings in their Newport mansions, such as the grand house party held by Mr. and Mrs. Alfred G. Vanderbilt in 1903. They also made time for charitable events. Mrs. Frederick W. Vanderbilt hosted an annual Thanksgiving Day dinner at the Masonic Hall for the newsboys and telegraph messengers of Newport, which often totaled over three hundred and was attended by the mayor and other prominent leaders.

The Breakers, Vanderbilt residence, Newport, Rhode Island NEW YORK PUBLIC LIBRARY

room for them to eat and play. This included a miniature version of the adult table, decorated with colorful chrysanthemums and the placement of food and utensils within easy reach. Their turkey was given to them on a separate platter, along with an "abundance of nuts, apples, oranges and wholesome confectionery." Typically one or two older children were assigned the role of supervising the younger ones.

Ebenezer Maxwell Mansion, Philadelphia, Pennsylvania

Roast Turkey

This recipe was originally featured in an 1885 issue of Godey's Lady's Book *with the description, "a more delicious way of cooking a turkey it is impossible to imagine." Its most unique aspect is the use of canned tomatoes to baste the bird, specified in the recipe as "a plump young turkey." During the Gilded Age, roast turkey was often garnished with celery tops, fried oysters, slices of ham, slices of lemon, fried sausages, or "forcemeat balls," an addition featured in this recipe adapted for modern palates by food historian and culinary stylist Dan Macey.*

SERVES 8–10

1 turkey, about 15 pounds
2 tablespoons all-purpose flour, plus 1 teaspoon
1 (28-ounce) can whole tomatoes
1 stick (½ cup) unsalted butter
1 teaspoon dried sage
1 teaspoon Italian seasoning
¼ teaspoon ground nutmeg
1 teaspoon salt
½ teaspoon pepper

Preheat oven to 400°F. Spray a large roasting pan with cooking spray.

Rinse the turkey thoroughly. Pat dry with paper towels and lightly dust with 2 tablespoons flour. Place the turkey in the roasting pan.

Heat the can of tomatoes and its juices in a saucepan over medium heat. Break up the tomatoes into smaller pieces with a knife or fork. Add the butter and continue to cook until the butter is melted. Add the sage, Italian seasoning, nutmeg, salt, pepper and 1 teaspoon flour and whisk until slightly thickened. Remove from heat.

Brush about one-third of the tomato mixture all over the turkey. Place in the oven for 15 minutes.

Turn down the heat to 350°F and baste again with one-third of the tomato mixture. Continue to roast until an internal thermometer reads 160°F, about 3–3½ hours. Be careful not to allow the top of the turkey to burn as the tomato turns to sugar. Lower the temperature or vent a large piece of aluminum foil over the top if this begins to occur before the bird is totally cooked.

Baste the bird a third time with the remaining tomato mixture and continue cooking until the thigh meat reaches 165°F. Remove the turkey from the oven and allow to rest for 20 minutes before carving. Serve on a platter garnished with the forcemeat balls and celery tops and accompanied by dressing.

Thanksgiving Dressing

Historically, dressing *was often a term used to indicate a bread and herb mixture that was cooked in a pan outside of the turkey cavity, while* stuffing *was cooked inside the bird. While the terms are interchangeable today, food historian and culinary stylist Dan Macey chose to adapt this recipe to be cooked outside of the bird. The original stuffing recipe in* Godey's Lady's Book *included half a pound of suet, which Dan tried to update using shortening, but even that produced a consistency that most would find too mealy today, so he opted for a combination of olive oil and chicken broth. He also retained the tomatoes in the original recipe for a unique period taste.*

SERVES 8–10

2 tablespoons olive oil
1 onion, chopped
2 celery stalks with green tops, chopped
2 carrots, peeled and diced
2 tablespoons chopped fresh parsley
1 teaspoon dried thyme
½ teaspoon ground cloves
½ teaspoon ground nutmeg
1 teaspoon salt
8 ounces sage-flavored sausage
1 (28-ounce) can whole tomatoes
8–10 cups day-old bread, cubed
3 cups chicken broth

Preheat oven to 350°F. Butter a shallow 2-quart casserole dish.

Heat the olive oil in a large skillet over medium heat. Add the chopped onions, celery, and carrots and cook until slightly wilted, about 4 minutes.

Add the parsley, thyme, cloves, nutmeg, and salt. Stir to combine, then add the sausage and continue to cook, breaking up the sausage until cooked through. Add the tomatoes and cook for another 5 minutes. Add the bread cubes and chicken broth and mix well.

Place the dressing in the casserole dish and bake for 35–45 minutes. Serve as an accompaniment to the roast turkey.

Chicken Forcemeat Balls

Adapted from Mrs. Rorer's New Cook Book *(1902) by food historian and culinary stylist Dan Macey, this dish is a nice accompaniment and garnish to the roast turkey. Forcemeat is a mixture of chopped and seasoned meat or vegetables for use as a stuffing or garnish.*

SERVES 8–10

2 cups milk
1 cup bread crumbs
3 egg yolks
1 tablespoon chopped parsley
1 teaspoon salt
⅛ teaspoon cayenne pepper
¼ teaspoon ground nutmeg
1 pound ground chicken

Preheat oven to 400°F.

Combine the milk and bread crumbs in a saucepan over medium heat. Stir until thick, then add the egg yolks. Remove from heat and mix in the parsley, salt, cayenne, nutmeg, and chicken.

When cool enough to handle, form into 1-inch balls and place on a large baking sheet lined with parchment paper. Bake for 25–30 minutes. Serve on the platter with the garnished turkey.

Sweet Potato Croquettes

Sweet potatoes have long been a staple side dish on American Thanksgiving tables. Their golden orange color and rich flavor meshes perfectly with the autumn season. And like turkey, pumpkin, and cranberries, they are one of the New World foods that were increasingly integrated into Thanksgiving menus as this celebratory meal gained in popularity. During the Gilded Age, they were often featured on Thanksgiving menus in croquette form. The recipe below was adapted from Delmonico chef Charles Ranhofer's cookbook The Epicurean. *To serve the croquettes, he recommended plating them in a circle, with sprigs of parsley embellishing the center.*

SERVES 4

2 large (or 4 medium) sweet potatoes (2 cups cooked)

1 egg yolk

2 tablespoons unsalted butter, softened

½ teaspoon salt

½ teaspoon ground nutmeg

1 large egg, slightly beaten

1 cup bread crumbs

¾–1 cup canola oil, for frying

Fresh parsley, for garnish

Rinse sweet potatoes and pierce in several places with a fork. Wrap each in a paper towel, place on a microwave-safe plate, and cook on high for 5 minutes in the microwave. Check for tenderness with a fork. If still not cooked through, continue to microwave in 1-minute intervals until tender. Remove from the microwave and allow to cool.

When cool, scrape out cooked sweet potato and place in a large mixing bowl. Add the egg yolk, butter, salt, and nutmeg, then mash with a potato masher until smooth. Chill in the refrigerator for 1 hour.

Place the beaten egg in a small bowl and the bread crumbs in a separate low dish (a pie plate works well). Using a cookie scoop or melon baller, shape the sweet potato mixture into 1-inch balls. Dip the sweet potato balls into the beaten egg mixture, then roll in the bread crumbs until completely covered.

Add the oil to a deep drying pan or skillet and place over medium-high heat. When the temperature reaches 350–370°F on a candy thermometer, add croquettes and fry until golden brown (about 2 minutes per side), working in batches. Drain on wire racks set on top of paper towels.

To serve, arrange on a large plate in a circle and garnish the center with sprigs of fresh parsley.

Crisp Celery

Today celery is mainly reserved for crudité platters or to add crunch to chicken or tuna salad, but it was actually considered a high-status food in the Gilded Age, mainly because it was rather difficult to cultivate. It had to be protected by piles of soil as it grew in order to preserve the whiteness and sweetness of its stalks. Common celery preparations included stewed, fried, braised, or dressed with mayonnaise. But it was also served raw, displayed in distinctive stands or vases made of cut glass or silver, particularly during special occasions such as Thanksgiving and Christmas. These fancy serving dishes could be tall and sturdy to hold the celery upright like a bouquet of flowers or shaped like a low basket or "boat" to cradle the celery lying down. According to Boston Cooking School instructor Maria Parloa, "celery should be scraped and washed and then put in ice water to be made crisp, at least an hour before it goes on the table."

SERVES 6–8

1 large head celery
White vinegar or lemon juice (optional)
Salt (optional)

Separate the celery stalks, removing any of the tough outer stalks, reserving for another use. Wash the stalks thoroughly and trim the bottom ends and any tough outer leaves. Place in a large basin filled with ice water for 1 hour, adding a few drops of vinegar or lemon juice if desired (this helps keep the celery crisp).

To serve, drain celery into a colander and pat dry with a dish towel. Arrange stalks in a celery vase or oval dish. Serve with little dishes of salt to sprinkle on the celery stalks if desired.

Pumpkin Cake

Pie is the traditional way to feature pumpkin on the Thanksgiving menu, but during the Gilded Age, pumpkin and other squashes also found their way into other desserts, including puddings, tarts, fritters, and cakes. Some of these were heartier, substituting cornmeal for flour, such as pumpkin loaf (similar to Boston brown bread) and pumpkin Indian pudding. But this recipe uses cake flour for a lighter, fancier cake that makes a pretty addition to the Thanksgiving table.

1 stick (½ cup) unsalted butter, softened
1 cup granulated sugar
1 cup packed brown sugar
2 large eggs, beaten
1 cup cooked (or canned) pumpkin
3 cups cake flour
4 teaspoons baking powder
¼ teaspoon baking soda
½ cup milk
1 cup chopped walnuts
1 teaspoon maple extract

Preheat oven to 350°F. Grease and flour two 9-inch round cake pans and set aside.

Beat butter in a large bowl with an electric mixer until creamy. Add granulated sugar, brown sugar, eggs, and pumpkin and mix well.

Sift together flour, baking powder, and baking soda. Add alternately with milk to the butter mixture. Fold in walnuts and maple extract.

Pour batter into cake pans and bake for 30–40 minutes. Cool on wire racks for 10 minutes and then remove from pans to cool completely. Frost with maple butter frosting.

MAPLE BUTTER FROSTING

6 tablespoons butter, softened
3½ cups confectioners' sugar
3 tablespoons milk
½ teaspoon vanilla extract
1 teaspoon maple extract

Combine all ingredients in a large mixing bowl. Beat with an electric mixer until creamy, adding another tablespoon of milk if necessary to achieve a good spreading consistency.

Baked Apple Pudding

A common nineteenth-century treat, this dessert was sometimes called Bird's Nest Pudding, since once the apples were baked, they resembled eggs in a nest. This "nest" varied from a cake-like batter or biscuit dough to a custard or even a piecrust. The recipe below is adapted from The White House Cookbook, *originally published in 1887 by Fanny Lemira Gillette. In later editions Mrs. Gillette collaborated with Hugo Ziemann, who was the White House steward from 1889 to 1891 under President Benjamin Harrison. Prior to this position, he had served as caterer for Prince Louis-Napoleon of France (the only son of Napoleon III) and the steward of hotels in Paris, New York, and Chicago. His contributions to the cookbook gave in-depth insight into White House cookery, including chapters on presidential dinner menus and management.*

SERVES 6–8

6 medium slightly tart apples, such as Granny Smith or Cortland
1 cup brown sugar
1 teaspoon cinnamon
½ teaspoon ground nutmeg
3 large eggs, separated
1½ cups all-purpose flour
2 teaspoons baking powder
½ teaspoon salt
1½ cups milk
2 cups heavy cream
½ cup confectioners' sugar

Preheat oven to 350°F. Grease a deep 2-quart baking dish with butter or cooking spray.

Peel and core the apples and arrange them inside the baking dish in a circular pattern.

Mix the brown sugar, cinnamon, and nutmeg together in a small bowl and then spoon into the apple cores. Bake for 20 minutes.

While the apples are baking, make the batter. In a glass or stainless steel bowl, beat the egg whites until firm, about 5–8 minutes, and set aside. In a separate large mixing bowl, beat the egg yolks until light. Sift the flour with the baking powder and salt and add to the egg yolks. Stir in the milk and mix well. Add the beaten egg whites and mix again.

Baked Apple Pudding

CONTINUED

Pour the mixture over the apples and bake for 45 minutes to 1 hour or until the crust is nicely browned and a toothpick inserted into the center comes out clean.

Make a sauce by combining the heavy cream and confectioners' sugar. To serve, scoop pudding into dessert bowls and pour sauce over each serving. Serve immediately.

NOTE: *The apples may release quite a bit of liquid during the cooking process, so do keep this in mind and go with as deep a dish as you can find.*

CHRISTMAS

Woolson Spice trade card, 1890 FLICKR COMMONS

Many of the Christmas traditions still celebrated today in America stem from those that became popular in the nineteenth century. The influx of huge numbers of immigrants from countries where Christmas was actively celebrated (particularly Germany) made a big impact on the American acceptance of Christmas. When Americans saw the British royal family gathered around a Christmas tree (Queen Victoria's husband, Prince Albert, was German), they quickly adopted the tradition of bringing a tree inside and decorating it, often referred to as "the pretty German toy." By the 1870s, Christmas was widely celebrated in the United States and had become a holiday centered on family, gift giving, and excessive eating. Food was one of the most important of all the Christmas rituals. Even Christmas tree decorations were typically edible, including fruits such as cherries, plums, strawberries, and peaches, as well as popular candies and confections, cornucopias filled with nuts, sugarplums, and gold eggcups filled with comfits, lozenges, and barley sugar (hard candies).

DEBUTANTE BALLS

Christmas week was a big occasion for Gilded Age debutante balls, particularly in large cities such as New York, Philadelphia, and Washington, DC. Some even held these coming out parties on Christmas Day, such as the grand tea US Army Paymaster General Alfred Bates and his wife, Caroline, held for their daughter Elizabeth in 1899. Their large house was decked out in holiday greenery, and a huge Christmas tree greeted guests as they entered the foyer. An evening ball for Elizabeth and her young friends followed the tea.

The Christmas Society

Active in New York clubs, real estate, and politics in the 1890s, Oliver Sumner Teall was a businessman and philanthropist whose social ties purportedly rivaled Ward McAllister's for society leadership. In 1891 he created the Christmas Society, a charity dedicated to donating toys to the poor children of New York. Members included John Jacob Astor, Frederick W. Vanderbilt, and William Rockefeller Jr. The organization invited children to Madison Square Garden, where they handed out toys, candy, apples, and gingerbread. However, the event was scrutinized by the press for the chaotic way it was carried out. With nearly 35,000 in attendance, there was supposedly a rush at the gates, with some children waiting for hours outside in the cold without receiving a gift, although Teall insisted the event was run smoothly. In any case, after two years the charity ended up facing a deficit, so Teall organized a ball at Madison Square Garden to help raise money for the organization through the sale of $5 admission tickets and $30 box seats. Featuring two orchestras, nonstop dancing, and an à la carte supper, it was attended by both New York society and prominent people from as far away as Virginia, Cincinnati, and New Orleans, bringing Teall and his charity out of debt.

The food served on Christmas Day was supposed to be rich, frivolous, delicious, and appealing to both children and adults—a tall order! As a result, Christmas dinner was one of the most carefully planned meals of the year for Gilded Age women. It was an extensive menu, featuring many of the same dishes that are still favorites today, such as roast turkey with stuffing, cranberry jelly, and sweet potatoes, as well as some not often seen on modern Christmas dinner tables, such as celery, peas served in turnip cups, deviled spaghetti, and plum pudding. Although turkey was the traditional roast, some families served roast pig or followed English tradition by serving roast beef or roast goose. Gilded Age Christmas menus ranged from a two-course affair with all the typical Christmas foods to ultra-fancy eight-course dinners that kicked off with oysters on the half shell and featured multiple meats or fish in addition to roast turkey, such as boiled salmon with egg sauce and roast squabs.

To pull off such a feast, Christmas morning was hectic for the lady of the house. The dining room was arranged as soon as breakfast was cleared away, with the table placed in the center of the room and covered with a spotless linen tablecloth. The center featured a tall fruit bowl filled with colorful, shiny apples, grapes, and oranges surrounded by Christmas ferns. Cut-glass or china dishes filled with bonbons, olives, and salted almonds were positioned around the edges. Extensive preparation was required in order for dinner to be served by 1:00 p.m. This included roasting the turkey, cooking items ahead to be reheated later, and prepping dishes to be finished at the last minute.

White House Christmas

President Grover Cleveland holds the famous distinction of being the only US president to serve two nonconsecutive terms in office (from 1885 to 1889 and 1893 to 1897). He is also the only president to get married inside the White House. His bride, Frances Folsom, was just twenty-one when they wed in the Blue Room in 1886, which makes her the youngest First Lady in US history.

In 1893, the first Christmas the Clevelands spent back in the White House for Grover's second term, Frances opted to have a quiet Christmas and enjoy the time with their two young daughters, Ruth and Esther. Their dinner was extensive, but not "fancy" as was sometimes the case when the White House hosted visitors on Christmas Day. The menu featured oysters, bouillon, roast turkey with cracker stuffing, boiled onions, jellied cranberries, mashed turnips, chicken patties, green salad, olives, fancy pastries, ices, fruits and nuts, pies, and coffee. Mrs. Cleveland was adored by the public and known for her kind and generous nature, which included giving money and personalized Christmas gifts to all the White House servants. She also made sure the Christmas menu included enough food for the servants to enjoy, laying out a feast in the servants' hall, complete with flowers and complimentary treats for them to take home.

Although the hostess had plenty to do in serving the dinner and making sure the different dishes were timed correctly, she also typically had waitstaff assistance to help ensure that she could fulfill her duties at the dining table. After the first course of oysters was served, she would ladle the soup (usually a clear bouillon or consommé) from a large tureen set on the table in front of her and waitstaff would pass the bowls to each guest, serving the most distinguished first. After the soup course, the deviled spaghetti was brought in on small plates, and the soup plates were removed. The roast turkey was then placed before the host to carve. While he was carving, the waitstaff brought in the sweet potato croquettes, peas, and cranberry jelly, which the hostess would pass to guests while the waitstaff was busy serving the turkey. After the turkey was passed, the waitstaff served the remaining vegetable dishes and then, if necessary, refilled the glasses and passed the bread. Then it was finally time to eat!

Christmas images from The Ideal Cook Book *by Allie R. Gregory, 1902* *FLICKR COMMONS*

When dinner was over, it was time for the meal's highpoint—the Christmas pudding. After being doused in a thick, sugary sauce (which usually included brandy or wine), the pudding was lit up and the flaming dish, garnished with a sprig of holly, was proudly brought to the table to close out the celebratory meal. This traditional Christmas dessert originated in medieval England as plum pottage (sometimes called plum porridge), which was more liquid, like a soup, and served at the beginning of a meal. Like most puddings of the time, it was meat-based, so the ingredients included chopped beef or mutton, onions, and/or other root vegetables, as well as dried plums (hence the name), bread crumbs as a thickener, and copious amounts of wine, herbs, and spices

Ward McAllister's New Year's Ball

New Year's Day was also a festive holiday during the Gilded Age. In New York, society members often hosted elaborate balls. One of the most famous was the New Year's Ball organized by Ward McAllister at Delmonico's in 1888. It was a subscription ball, meaning one hundred gentlemen "subscribers" from New York society each paid $50 to fund the affair and were given seven invitations to distribute. The entire restaurant was reserved for this private event, which was attended by around seven hundred people.

Delmonico's Restaurant, Fifth Avenue, Broadway and 26th Street, 1893 WIKIMEDIA COMMONS

A cotillon dance led by businessman Thomas H. Howard and Emily Ladenburg (wife of financier Adolph Ladenberg) was held in the room known as the red parlor. The room was lavishly decorated with a new dance floor, potted palms, and expensive antique tapestries, which McAllister claimed were sent from Paris. Sheaves of wheat, palmetto, yellow roses, and holly lined the walls, a striking contrast to the crimson background. Another cotillon was held in the ballroom, led by lawyer Lispenard Stewart and Alice Vanderbilt. Here the color scheme was pink, white, and shades of red. Clematis and feathery Japanese vines were draped between the mirrors, and ornamental pots filled with blooming plants were scattered around the room. Palms and scarlet poinsettias provided bright pops of color on the balcony where the musicians were performing. A side room to the ballroom was transformed into a balmy conservatory of rare orchids, palms, and tree ferns.

The ladies' cloak room was converted into a Japanese tearoom serving little cakes, lemonade, and wine punch. Supper was served in the restaurant and café rooms at 12:45 a.m., led by McAllister and Oliva Cutting (wife of lawyer and financier William Bayard Cutting). The menu included canvasback duck, pâté de foie gras, and other delicacies, paired with four kinds of Champagne. In his book, *Society as I Have Found It*, McAllister claimed the New Year's Ball surpassed anything he had given previously.

for flavor. This rich dish was a favorite for feast days such as All Saints Day, Christmas, and New Year's Day, but it wasn't until the 1600s that it became specifically associated with Christmas, and the name changed to the more luxurious-sounding plum pudding or even Christmas pudding. Over the years, the meat was replaced by suet (the protective fat around the kidneys of beef or mutton) and the vegetables were gradually phased out, although some cooks still include a token carrot in their version.

Plum Pudding Trade Card, nineteenth century
NEW YORK PUBLIC LIBRARY

Newport's New Year's Ball

Two years after Ward McAllister's grand New Year's Ball, real estate magnate William R. Hunter organized a similar event for Newport's winter society members. Like McAllister's ball, it was also a subscription affair that collected numerous sign-ups, ensuring it was "successful financially as well as socially," as per the *New York Times*. It was held in Newport's Masonic Hall, which was decorated with drapes of Christmas greenery, Christmas trees in every corner, and numerous tropical plants. Velvet curtains framed the windows, and one corner was transformed into a cozy nook with elegant tapestries, plush furniture, and soft lighting. Hunter led the cotillon dance, which kicked off at 10:00 p.m. Located in a separate part of the hall, the extravagant dining table was enclosed by curtains to hide it from view, unveiled with fanfare when supper was announced. Guests included several army and navy officers, Mr. and Mrs. Walter L. Kane (from the Astor family), Mr. and Mrs. Fairman Rogers (a civil engineer and professor), and many other notables from Newport society.

Steamed Halibut with Egg Sauce

Fish was often featured on Gilded Age holiday menus, particularly those that were multi-course affairs. Since these dinners were designed to transition into more substantial dishes as the courses progressed, the fish would have been served after the soup course and prior to the roast (turkey, goose, or beef). Halibut, salmon, and cod were among the favorite fish types available during the Christmas season. The fish was typically baked or steamed and served with a rich lobster or egg sauce. An 1899 Boston Cooking School Magazine *article recommends reserving a little of the butter and then melting and mixing it into the egg sauce "just before it is sent to the table" to give the fish an extra burst of buttery flavor.*

SERVES 4

1 (2–3 pound) piece of halibut
¼ teaspoon salt
⅛ teaspoon white pepper
Fresh parsley, for garnish

FOR THE EGG SAUCE:
3 tablespoons butter
2 tablespoons all-purpose flour
2 cups milk
¼ teaspoon salt
Dash of white pepper
3 hard-boiled eggs, sliced and chopped

Sprinkle halibut with salt and pepper and then set aside. Place a steamer basket inside a large pot, then fill the pot about halfway with water and bring to a boil. Place the halibut inside the steamer basket and cook for 7–10 minutes or until the fish reaches 130°F. Remove to a platter and keep warm.

Make the egg sauce by melting the butter in a medium saucepan over medium heat. Add the flour, whisking constantly until a paste forms. Add the milk, salt, and pepper, stirring vigorously until the mixture thickens to a creamy consistency. Add the hard-boiled eggs and turn the heat down to low until just heated through.

Pour some of the egg sauce over the fish and add the rest to a gravy boat for serving at the table. Garnish the fish with sprigs of fresh parsley and serve immediately.

Peas Served in Turnip Cups

This dish was often served during the vegetable course at Gilded Age Christmas dinners. The contrast of the green peas against the white background of the turnips added a festive pop of color to the holiday table. Some cookbooks from the era suggest adding a tablespoon of sugar to the water when cooking the turnips to counteract any bitterness. Feel free to try this step if you like.

SERVES 4

FOR THE TURNIPS:

4 small white turnips

1 teaspoon salt

1 teaspoon sugar (optional)

Parsley, for garnish

FOR THE PEAS:

1 cup peas, fresh or frozen

¼ teaspoon salt

⅛ teaspoon pepper

FOR THE CREAM SAUCE:

1 tablespoon butter

1 teaspoon all-purpose flour

2 tablespoons cream or milk

Wash and peel the turnips. Place in a large pot with 6 cups of water, salt and sugar (if using) and bring to a boil over high heat, then turn down to medium-low and cook for 25–30 minutes until fork tender.

While the turnips are cooking, fill a large bowl with ice water. When the turnips are done, drain and immediately place in the bowl of ice water for 1 minute to stop the cooking process. Remove to a cutting board. When cool enough to handle, scoop out the turnip centers with a spoon or melon baller. Set aside.

Place the peas and ½ cup water in a small saucepan and bring to a boil over high heat. Reduce heat to medium, uncover, and cook 4–6 minutes or until just tender. When done, sprinkle with salt and pepper and set aside.

Make a cream sauce by melting butter in a small saucepan over medium-high heat. Add flour and stir to form a paste. Add cream or milk and whisk until smooth.

Mix the cream sauce with the peas and then spoon into turnip cups. Arrange turnip cups on a small platter and garnish with parsley.

Deviled Spaghetti

This delicious dish is reminiscent of macaroni and cheese, swapping diced hard-boiled eggs for the cheese. It was a practical addition to the Christmas table, as it could be prepared ahead of time and then reheated in the oven just before dinner was served. It's not clear how the name originated, but it is likely from the cayenne pepper and chili sauce, which give it a kick and add a bit of holiday color.

SERVES 6

8 ounces (½ package) spaghetti or macaroni

2 tablespoons butter

2 tablespoons all-purpose flour

1 cup milk

3 hard-boiled eggs, sliced and chopped

½ teaspoon salt

¼ teaspoon cayenne pepper

1 teaspoon onion powder

⅛ teaspoon ground nutmeg

1 tablespoon chopped parsley

½ cup bread crumbs

1 tablespoon unsalted butter, melted

Chili sauce (optional)

Preheat oven to 350°F. Butter six ramekins or Texas-size muffin pans and set aside.

Cook the spaghetti until al dente, about 10 minutes. Drain and allow to cool. When cool, chop finely and set aside.

Melt the butter in a large saucepan over medium heat. Add the flour and whisk together to form a paste. Add the milk and bring to a boil, stirring constantly. Turn down to low and add the chopped eggs, salt, cayenne, onion powder, nutmeg, and parsley.

Add the spaghetti to the sauce, stirring until combined. Using a large ladle, divide spaghetti mixture among the ramekins or muffin pan cups.

Mix bread crumbs and melted butter in a small bowl. Spoon on top of spaghetti.

Transfer to the oven and bake for 30 minutes until tops are nicely browned. Remove from the oven and set on a wire rack to cool for at least 10 minutes. When cool, remove from the muffin pan by running a knife around the edges and carefully turning out onto a plate. If using ramekins, serve in the individual ramekin dishes.

Make an indentation in the top of each with the back of a spoon and add a teaspoon of chili sauce if desired. Serve immediately.

Lemon Star Cookies

Lemon was a popular dessert flavoring in the Gilded Age, sometimes used interchangeably with rose-water, orange flower water, or vanilla. Although sour by itself, when paired with butter, sugar, and eggs, it creates a taste sensation that is tangy and pleasantly astringent. This cookie's star shape makes it a festive Christmastime treat.

MAKES 4½ DOZEN

1½ sticks (¾ cup) unsalted butter, softened
1 cup sugar
1 large egg
3 cups all-purpose flour
3 teaspoons baking powder
½ teaspoon salt
2 tablespoons lemon juice
1 teaspoon lemon zest

Preheat oven to 375°F.

Using an electric mixer, cream the butter and sugar together, then beat in the egg.

Sift the flour, baking powder, and salt together, then slowly add to the wet ingredients. Stir in the lemon juice and zest and continue to mix until a soft dough forms.

Roll the dough out on a floured surface to a thickness of a little less than ¼ inch and cut into star shapes.

Place on parchment paper–lined baking sheets and bake for 8–10 minutes. Cool for a few minutes and then transfer to wire racks to cool completely.

When the cookies are completely cool, decorate with lemon icing or simply sprinkle with confectioners' sugar.

LEMON ICING

1 egg white
2 cups sifted confectioners' sugar
1 teaspoon lemon juice

Place all the ingredients in a medium mixing bowl. Beat using an electric mixer on high speed until firm. The icing should be of a soft enough consistency to flow through a fine pastry tube. Add a few more drops of lemon juice or water to obtain this consistency if needed.

Gâteaux de Milan

In the nineteenth century, these fashionable little cakes were often made in tandem with Swiss Penny Cakes, which were about the size of a Swiss penny. The two were a perfect combination since the Swiss Penny Cakes called for egg whites and the Gâteaux de Milan required egg yolks. This is a deliciously buttery cookie with a hint of lemon—simple, delectable elegance. In France, they are often featured during the Christmas season. Some recipes call for Cognac or rum, others for milk or cream. Use whatever tickles your fancy!

2 sticks (1 cup) salted butter, softened

1 cup sugar

2 eggs, yolks and whites separated

2–3 tablespoons milk or cream, or 1–2 tablespoons Cognac or rum

Zest from 1 lemon

3 cups all-purpose flour, sifted

Granulated or colored decorating sugar (optional)

Preheat oven to 375°F. Line two baking sheets with parchment paper and set aside.

Cream the butter and sugar, then add the egg yolks, your liquid of choice, and lemon zest. Mix well. Slowly add the flour until thoroughly incorporated. Chill dough for 1 hour.

Knead dough lightly on a floured surface and roll out to a thickness of a little less than ¼ inch. Add a bit more flour if dough still seems sticky. Cut into shapes with cookie cutters, glaze with beaten egg whites, and place on baking sheets.

Bake for 10–15 minutes. Cookies will spread during baking. Trim any burned edges by placing the cookie cutter over the cookie and pressing down to trim. Sprinkle with granulated or colored decorating sugar, if desired.

Plum Pudding

Plum pudding was the highlight of the Gilded Age holiday feast. It was a rich dessert containing suet (the protective fat around the kidneys of beef or mutton), dried fruit, and spices such as cinnamon, nutmeg, and cloves, as well as any combination of nuts, lemon or orange peel, chopped apple, flour, eggs, sugar, and milk, cider, or liquor. A sauce made from rum or brandy butter (sometimes called hard sauce) was often added right before serving. This version is based on temperance-movement recipes popular at the time.

MAKES 1 BUNDT PAN SIZED PUDDING OR 2 SMALLER ONES, SERVING 15–20 PEOPLE

2¾ cups raisins
1½ cups dried currants
½ cup candied ginger, chopped
½ cup dried pineapple, chopped
½ cup almonds, chopped
1 cup sugar
1¾ cups all-purpose flour
1¾ cups bread crumbs (preferably from egg bread such as challah or French brioche)
6 large eggs, beaten
1½ cups suet (or lard)
1 cup brandy (or apple cider)
Juice and zest from 1 orange
Juice and zest from 1 lemon
1 small whole nutmeg, grated
1 teaspoon allspice
1 teaspoon ground cinnamon
Pinch of salt

Mix all the ingredients together in a large bowl. Cover with plastic wrap and place in the refrigerator overnight.

The next day, stir batter again to make sure ingredients are well mixed. Coat a tin mold or Bundt pan with cooking spray and line with parchment paper. Pour mixture into the mold and cover with foil.

To steam the pudding, place a steamer insert or some crumbled aluminum foil in the bottom of a deep stockpot, then place the mold on top so that it is not touching the bottom. Fill the pot with enough water so that it is two-thirds up the sides. Bring the water to a boil, then lower it to a simmer, placing the lid on top. Steam the pudding for 4–5 hours, adding water if necessary.

Plum Pudding

Remove the pudding from the pot and cool for 1 hour on a wire rack. When cool, loosen the edges and carefully turn out onto a plate.

You can also steam the pudding in a crock pot. Add some water to cover the bottom of the crock pot, place the mold inside, and close the lid. Steam the pudding for 4–5 hours on high, then take it out and let it cool for 1 hour on a wire rack. When cool, loosen the edges and carefully turn out onto a plate.

Just before serving, make a hard sauce. Pour the sauce over the pudding and then cut in slices to serve.

HARD SAUCE

2 teaspoons cornstarch
2 tablespoons water
2 egg yolks
¼ cup sugar
1 cup milk
1 tablespoon apricot jelly
Pinch of ground nutmeg

Mix cornstarch and water in a small bowl until smooth, then whisk in egg yolks.

Heat sugar and milk in a medium saucepan over medium-high heat. When it begins to boil, turn down to low and add egg yolks and cornstarch, stirring briskly with a whisk to avoid scrambling. Stir until thick and creamy, then take off the burner and mix in jelly and nutmeg.

Sugar Plums

Sugar plums originated as small round or oval sweets made out of colored and boiled sugar, similar to what we think of today as hard candy. They resembled plums in size and shape and often had little wire stalks that could be used to hang them up as a festive decoration. By the Gilded Age, the term sugar plum *was used to describe small plum-shaped confections made from a mixture of chopped dried fruits, nuts, confectioners' sugar, and brandy (which served as a preservative). The recipe below calls for figs, dates, and apricots, but you can use any combination of dried fruits—soft candied cherries and citron were favorites during the late nineteenth century.*

2 cups finely chopped figs
2 cups finely chopped pitted dates
2 cups finely chopped apricots
2 cups chopped nuts
2 tablespoons brandy
Confectioners' sugar

Mix dried fruits, nuts, and brandy in a large bowl. Slowly add confectioners' sugar until mixture binds together.

Shape into bite-size balls and then roll in more confectioners' sugar. Store in an airtight container in the refrigerator for up to 2 weeks.

NOTE: *Wrapping each ball in colored plastic wrap or paper and tying with a ribbon also makes a lovely Christmas tree decoration.*

TWELFTH NIGHT

Twelfth Night Games, featured in St. Nicholas *(children's magazine), 1873* FLICKR COMMONS

Twelfth Night has traditionally been celebrated by Christians on January 6, or the Feast of Epiphany, representing the day when the Three Kings arrived in Bethlehem to give their gifts to baby Jesus. Gilded Age society often marked the occasion with a Twelfth Night party where they feasted on rich food and children were given three gifts (representing one from each wise man). Party décor was similar to other yuletide decorations, including evergreen garlands and wreaths of holly tied with colorful ribbons, accented by the addition of some colorful potted plants and fresh cut flowers. Chandeliers were often interwoven with festive vines and flowers.

A typical Twelfth Night supper began with oysters (either raw or creamed), followed by cream of clam soup, sandwiches cut in fancy shapes, fried chicken, potato balls, peas in rice cups, celery salad on lettuce leaves, fruit, candies, bonbons, and ice cream. Sometimes the meal followed a theme, such as a chafing dish supper or oyster roast, accompanied by coffee and cider. Chafing dish suppers were very popular in the latter part of the Gilded Age, starting in the 1890s. For these suppers, menu items were placed in fancy silver dishes kept warm over an alcohol lamp.

But the highlight of these Twelfth Night celebrations was the elaborately decorated Twelfth Night Cake. This was a large dense cake that was either similar to a pound cake or flavored with fruit, nuts, and spices like a fruitcake. A pea, a bean, and a clove were placed inside the cake. When it was served, whoever got the piece with the pea became the queen of the evening, whoever got the bean was the king, and the person receiving the slice with the clove was the jester. These three guests were allowed to preside over the evening activities, with the rest of the guests filling the "roles" of maids of honor and ministers of state. This often involved a coronation ceremony where the king and queen were crowned and then led the first dance and/or a series of toasts

Twelfth Night Performances

New York social clubs often included performances of Shakespeare's romantic comedy *Twelfth Night* in their Gilded Age Twelfth Night celebrations. In 1901, the Twentieth Century Club ushered in the new century with a lavish Twelfth Night event featuring a short skit of the play performed by club members including painter Alice Chittenden and Grace Newton Dana, wife of newspaper editor Arnold Guyot Dana. It was held at the Clinton Avenue home of businessman and Pratt Institute founder Charles Pratt, where a temporary stage was set up in the drawing room. When the play was over, guests proceeded into the dining room for supper, with the last one carrying a boar's head on a plate. After dinner the guests danced a Virginia reel, accompanied by live music from a string band.

Then in 1903, lawyer Charles W. Gould hosted a similar party given by the Omnibus Club in his Washington Square home. One act of Shakespeare's *Twelfth Night* was presented, featuring performances by Broadway actor Edward Fales Coward and investment banker William Stackpole. The play was followed by dancing, games, and wassail. A more inclusive version of the "Four Hundred," the Omnibus Club was formed to keep New York society together and increase membership. Its annual parties were often hosted in the 16th Street studio of Howard and Steven Constable, brothers who established an architecture and engineering firm with offices in New York and Philadelphia.

with cups of punch. Sometimes festivities began early in the day and continued through midnight. Party activities included fun events like a magic or puppet show and parlor games such as a bean-bag toss and charades. Other times the party took the form of a costume ball, with dancing followed by supper.

At the end of the evening, all the Christmas greens were taken down and burned on the Yule log to prevent bad fortune in the coming year. The king or queen would have the honor of placing the last wreath on the fire, making the request that everyone banish prior grudges and have a year filled with peace and harmony. A "loving cup" of grape juice, fruit punch, or mulled cider was passed around for all to take a sip and make a wish for the new year.

Twelfth Night Cake

During the Gilded Age, it was customary to bake Twelfth Night Cake in a ring-shaped mold. Once it was iced, red and white candles were often placed on the top to form a five-pointed star shape and sprigs of fresh holly were added as a garnish, creating a wreath-like appearance. This recipe calls for adding the bean, pea, and clove after the cake is baked but before it is frosted. Once the cake is cut, the person who receives the piece with the bean gets to be the king for the evening, the person who receives the piece with the pea gets to be the queen, and the person who gets the clove is the court jester.

SERVES 12–16

3½ cups cake flour
3 teaspoons baking powder
½ teaspoon salt
2 sticks (1 cup) unsalted butter, softened
2 cups sugar
5 large egg yolks, separated individually (reserve egg whites)
½ cup orange juice
½ cup milk
3 egg whites
1 dried bean, 1 dried black-eye pea, and 1 clove
Red and white candles and fresh holly, for garnish (optional)

Preheat oven to 350°F. Grease and flour a 10-inch tube pan and set aside.

Sift flour, baking powder, and salt in a large bowl.

In a separate bowl, cream butter using an electric mixer on medium-high speed until smooth. Gradually add the sugar, beating until light and fluffy, scraping down the sides of the bowl if necessary. Add the egg yolks one at a time, beating after each addition. Turn mixer speed to low and add flour alternately with orange juice and milk.

In a separate glass or stainless steel bowl, beat egg whites on low speed until foamy, about 3–4 minutes, then increase speed to medium and continue to beat another 5–8 minutes or until stiff. Fold into the batter (best done by hand).

Transfer the batter to the tube pan and bake for 1 hour or until a toothpick inserted into the center comes out clean. Cool for 10 minutes on a wire rack, then place another rack on top and carefully flip the cake. It should slide out of the pan onto the rack.

Twelfth Night Cake

Remove the bottom of the tube pan. Insert the bean, pea, and clove into different parts of the cake. Allow it to cool completely before frosting with royal icing.

ROYAL ICING

2 egg whites

2 teaspoons lemon juice

3¼ cups confectioners' sugar, sifted

Whisk egg whites on low speed until foamy, about 4–5 minutes, then stir in lemon juice. Add confectioners' sugar a little at a time, increasing speed to medium-high until icing is smooth and glossy.

BIBLIOGRAPHY

"Afternoon Tea Room: Gothamites Will Be Treated to a Real Novelty This Winter." *New York Times*, October 13, 1896.

"Banquets of the Season Whose Flavor Lingers in the Memory." *New York Times*, May 24, 1908.

Bartholomew, Duane P., Richard A. Hawkins, and Johnny A. Lopez. "Hawaii Pineapple: The Rise and Fall of an Industry." *HortScience* 47, no. 10 (2012): 1390–98. https://doi.org/10.21273/HORTSCI.47.10.1390.

Bianculli, Anthony J. *Trains and Technology: The American Railroad in the Nineteenth Century.* Vol. 2, *Cars.* Newark: University of Delaware Press, 2002.

"Billings Threw His Coin Away." *Buffalo Enquirer*, March 30, 1903.

"Booths, Beauty and Booty." *New York Herald*, December 4, 1887.

"A Bride at the White House." *New-York Tribune*, February 18, 1906.

Bridenbaugh, Carl, and Jessica Bridenbaugh. *Rebels and Gentlemen: Philadelphia in the Age of Franklin.* Westport, CT: Greenwood Press, 1978.

Burrows, Edwin G., and Mike Wallace. *Gotham: A History of New York City to 1898*. New York: Oxford University Press, 1999.

Clark, Jean Wilde, ed. *Weddings and Wedding Anniversaries: A Book of Good Form in the Conduct of Marriage Ceremonies*. New York: Butterick Publishing Company, 1910.

Cooke, Maud C. *Social Etiquette; or, Manners and Customs of Polite Society.* London, ON: McDermid & Logan, 1896.

"The Cooking Academy—Seventh Lecture." *Cincinnati Enquirer*, April 19, 1865.

"Cooking as a Fad." *Oshkosh Northwestern*, October 30, 1897.

Cooper, Lenna. "The Hospital Dietitian Arrives." *The Trained Nurse and Hospital Review*, May 1938.

Crain, Esther. *The Gilded Age in New York, 1870–1910*. New York: Black Dog & Leventhal Publishers, 2016.

Dean, C. *The World's Fair City and Her Enterprising Sons*. Chicago: United Publishing Company, 1892.

"Delmonico's Restaurant: Opening of the New House—Sketch of Some of the Famous Dinners Given at the Old Fourteenth Street Establishment." *New York Times*, September 14, 1876.

De Voe, Thomas Farrington. *The Market Assistant: Containing a Brief Description of Every Article of Human Food Sold in the Public Markets of the Cities of New York, Boston, Philadelphia, and Brooklyn; Including the Various Domestic and Wild Animals, Poultry, Game, Fish, Vegetables, Fruits etc. with Many Curious Incidents and Anecdotes.* New York: Hurd and Houghton, 1867.

"The Dickens Banquet." *New York Times*, April 19, 1968.

"The Doings of Women Folk." *Times Union* (Albany, NY), September 7, 1889.

Dudden, Faye E. *Serving Women: Household Service in Nineteenth-Century America*. 1st ed. Middletown, CT: Wesleyan University Press, 1983.

"Events of the Week." *New York Times*, October 24, 1897.

"Fanny Lemira Gillette." Feeding America: The Historic American Cookbook Project. Michigan State University Libraries Digital Repository. Accessed July 15, 2022. https://d.lib.msu.edu/content/biographies?author_name=Gillette%2C+F.+L.+%28Fanny+Lemira%29%2C+1828-1926.

Farmer, Fannie Merritt. *Fannie Farmer's Book of Good Dinners.* Princeton, NJ: Pyne Press, 1972.

Grimes, William. *Appetite City: A Culinary History of New York.* New York: Farrar, Straus and Giroux, 2013.

Grover, Kathryn. *Dining in America, 1850–1900*. Amherst: University of Massachusetts Press, 1987.

Haley, Andrew P. *Turning the Tables: The Aristocratic Restaurant and the Rise of the American Middle Class, 1880–1920*. Chapel Hill: University of North Carolina Press, 2011.

"History of Lakewood." Township of Lakewood website. Accessed July 13, 2022. https://www.lakewoodnj.gov/history.

Homberger, Eric. *Mrs. Astor's New York: Money and Social Power in a Gilded Age*. New Haven, CT: Yale University Press, 2004.

"The International Sleeping Car Company of Europe." *Railroad Gazette*, June 9, 1899.

Lakewood Survey. State of New Jersey website. Accessed July 13, 2022. https://www.nj.gov/dep/hpo/hrrcn_sandy_OCE_GB_147_148_PDF/OCE_GB_148_v15.pdf.

Lobel, Cindy R. *Urban Appetites: Food and Culture in Nineteenth-Century New York.* Chicago: University of Chicago Press, 2015.

McAllister, Ward. *Society as I Have Found It.* New York: Cassell Publishing Company, 1890.

McLaws, Lafayette. "Girls Interests and Occupations." *The Delineator*, November 1898.

Megee, Katherine E. "A Fourth of July Tea." *Table Talk*, July 1908.

Nordoff, Charles. "California: How to Go There, and What to See by the Way." *Harpers New Monthly Magazine*, May 1872.

Pairpoint, Alfred J. *Rambles in America, Past and Present*. Boston: A. Mudge & Son, printers, 1891.

Peterson, Carla L. *Black Gotham: A Family History of African Americans in Nineteenth-Century New York City*. New Haven, CT: Yale University Press, 2011.

Porterfield, James D. *Dining by Rail: The History and the Recipes of America's Golden Age of Railroad Cuisine.* New York: St. Martin's Press, 1993.

"Pullman Dining Cars: A Trial Trip on the English Midland Railway." *New York Times,* July 19, 1882.

"Pullman Loaves." The Food Timeline. Accessed March 27, 2022. www.foodtimeline.org/foodbreads.html.

Quinzio, Jeri. *Food on the Rails: The Golden Era of Railroad Dining*. Lanham, MD: Rowman & Littlefield, 2014

———. *Of Sugar and Snow: A History of Ice Cream Making*. Berkeley: University of California Press, 2009.

"A Realistic Supper." *Buffalo Evening News*, February 2, 1888.

Rorer, Sarah Tyson (Heston). *Mrs. Rorer's Every Day Menu Book*. Philadelphia: Arnold and Company, 1905.

———. "A Pair of Wedding Breakfasts." *Ladies Home Journal*, April 1894.

Ross, Christopher. "Mint Julep: The Origins of the Derby's Official Drink." CNN, September 4, 2020. https://www.cnn.com/travel/article/cocktail-history-mint-julep-kentucky-derby/index.html.

Sala, George Augustus. *America Revisited: From the Bay of New York to the Gulf of Mexico, and from Lake Michigan to the Pacific*. London: Vizetelly & Company, 1882.

Sangster, Margaret Elizabeth. *Good Manners for All Occasions: A Practical Manual*. New York: Christian Herald, 1904.

Shapiro, Laura. *Perfection Salad: Women and Cooking at the Turn of the Century*. Berkeley: University of California Press, 2009.

Shrock, Joel. *The Gilded Age*. Westport, CT: Greenwood Press, 2004.

Smiley, James Bethuel. *Modern Manners and Social Forms: A Manual of the Manners and Customs of the Best Modern Society, Comp. from the Latest Authorities.* Chicago: James B. Smiley, 1890.

Smith, Andrew F. *Peanuts: The Illustrious History of the Goober Pea.* Urbana: University of Illinois Press, 2002

———. *New York City: A Food Biography*. Lanham, MD: Rowman & Littlefield, 2013.

———, ed. *Oxford Companion to American Food and Drink*. New York: Oxford University Press, 2007.

———, ed. *Savoring Gotham: A Food Lover's Companion to New York City.* New York: Oxford University Press, 2015.

Stevens, Frances. *The Usages of the Best Society: A Complete Manual of Social Etiquette*. New York: A. L. Burt, 1884.

"Teach Them How to Cook: Illinois Women Open a Room at the Fair in a Practical Manner." *Inter Ocean* (Chicago, IL), May 11, 1893.

Townsend, Grace. *Dining Room and Kitchen: An Economical Guide in Practical Housekeeping for the American Housewife, Containing the Choicest Tried and Approved Cookery Recipes*. New York: Home Publishing Co., 1902.

"Trade News." *American Stationer*, July 16, 1885.

"Ugly Club Annual Dinner. A Feast of Reason and a Flow of Soul." *New York Globe*, January 6, 1883.

Vosburgh, W. S. "The Passing of Jerome Park." *Outing*, April 1901.

Whitehead, Jessup. *The Steward's Handbook and Guide to Party Catering*. Chicago: J. Anderson & Co., 1889.

"Will Duplicate Her Wedding Expenses to Charitable Work." *Kansas City Journal*, April 5, 1899.

Williams, Susan. *Food in the United States, 1820s–1890*. Westport, CT: Greenwood Press, 2006.

———. *Savory Suppers and Fashionable Feasts: Dining in Victorian America*. Knoxville: University of Tennessee Press, 1996.

RECIPE INDEX

ACKNOWLEDGMENTS

I am extremely grateful to each and every person who contributed to this cookbook. It was an honor and privilege to collaborate with photographer Heather Raub of Front Room Images and culinary stylist Dan Macey of dantasticfood. We formed a cohesive team, freely sharing thoughts, skills, and ideas. I am so appreciative to them both for their talent and expertise. This book would not have happened without their creative influences!

A big thank you to my agent, Linda Konner, for her constant support, perseverance, and guidance and my Globe Pequot editor, Amy Lyons, for her vision and confidence in this project. I am also indebted to Chef Walter Staib, host and executive producer of *A Taste of History*, for both referring me to Linda and writing such a lovely and eloquent foreword. Our shared appreciation of historic recipes and food history has been an immensely rewarding connection.

Making sure the photographs were historically appropriate was also a group effort. Many of the dishes and recipes were contributions from my mom, Mary Ellsworth Libourel. It was a dream come true to be able to use family heirlooms and see them photographed so beautifully. I'd also like to express my gratitude to Heather Raub's friends Dick and MaryBeth Currie. They loaned us period tableware from Dick's grandparents, John A. and Julia G. Currie. Married in 1893, the Curries lived in a three-story brownstone in West Philadelphia (now the "University City" section of the city) from 1906 until the early 1930s. John was the founding president of the former Energy Elevator Company in Philadelphia (1887–1978). It was a pleasure to be able to showcase these gorgeous pieces. I am also grateful to Dan Macey for his huge supply of historic props and gifted ability to style the food in such an accurate and attractive way.

I am extremely appreciative for the opportunity to take photographs at two historical locations: the Ebenezer Maxwell Mansion in Philadelphia and the restored Pullman Dining Cars and Rod's Steak & Seafood Grille restaurant inside the Madison Hotel in Morristown, New Jersey. Both of these places brought such vivid authenticity to the photographs. Many thanks to both Diane Richardson, Ebenezer Maxwell's director, and Jerry Keller, restaurant manager of the Madison Hotel, for giving us the liberty to use these settings and their historic backgrounds.

Thank you also to Heather Raub and the Straube Building in Pennington for letting us do two days of food photography and styling in Heather's studio, which included a visit from the local fire department. (I'll leave it at that, ha ha!) Thanks to Heather's photographer friend and colleague Dan Komoda for sharing thoughts and opinions on some of the photos, and to Barbara Rothwell Henderson, owner of the Flower Shop of Pennington Market, for providing a beautiful ribbon to embellish the charlotte russe dessert.

Sincere gratitude to Dan Macey and his husband Paul Savidge for allowing us to use their lovely Chestnut Hill home for some of the photographs. I couldn't have asked for a more perfect setting! Also a huge thank you to Dan for all his editorial assistance—from writing sidebars, text, and recipes to reading chapters and offering thoughts and feedback. His opinions were truly valuable and made the book more polished. Thanks also go out to Chef Adam Diltz of Elwood Restaurant in Philadelphia for his recipe contribution of Rabbit, Hunter Style.

A cookbook cannot be complete without recipe testing, and I would like to thank my husband, Joe Diamond, and children, Cate and Patrick Diamond, for tasting many recipes, giving their honest opinion, and providing constant support. Cate also lent her artistic talents to help make and decorate some of the desserts for various photo shoots. And a shout-out to my good friends Bruce, Laura, India, and Henry Franklin, Carol DeSerio, Calli Lambard, Andy and Chris Liddie, Eileen Reilly, and Kerry Franklin for being taste testers at our many dinners. Feedback from all of you helped make the recipes better!

ABOUT THE AUTHOR

Becky Libourel Diamond is a food writer, librarian, and research historian. She has been writing about food since 2008, parlaying her passion for food and history into the publication of *The Thousand Dollar Dinner* and *Mrs. Goodfellow: The Story of America's First Cooking School*. She has also written about food and history for *Eaten Magazine*, *Newtown Lifestyle*, Dianne Jacob's *Will Write for Food* blog, *BookPage*, *Table Matters: The Journal of Food, Drink and Manners, The Historical Cooking Project*, *IFIS Food and Health Information*, Rutgers University's *Books We Read* blog, Prose Media, and Philadelphia's Mütter Museum. She lives in Yardley, Pennsylvania.